Drinking from Mimir's Well
By Dave Migman

The contents of this book, both writing
and artwork, are the author's own work.
This work is Copyright 2020 Dave Migman

Many Thanks to Steph for taking
the role of editor
and supplying epic enthusiasm.

SEEPING i PRESS

Introduction

When I began this research, I had in mind creating a simple runic reference book for interested people - the research growing from studies for a story called King Oddr. However the deeper I delved the more profound the runes became. I wanted to search through the layers of time to discover kernels of wisdom, directly contemporary with the Germanic tribal era when the use of runes developed. I soon realised that such an endeavour is impossible. Time, and many hands, have occluded much of the original meanings. Christian monks/ scribes filtered out much that was no doubt too 'heathen' for their tastes. Similarly, in the seventies, New Age writers filtered out the harsher, negative connotations of many symbols to fit with their world view. The process of change and assimilation is timeless.

I have collected as much relevant Germanic/ Norse material as I could - to present a slightly hardened companion to the rune book of your choice. There are many books out there, some better than others, but I hope armed with this little tome you might be able to gain additional insight into each symbol. It must be remembered that when dealing with runes, powerful symbolism acts as a root, but much has been altered, and is still being altered, with the flavour of the times. Unfortunately much of our understanding comes from scant information. The tiniest morsel can yield many interpretations. Today, divorced as we are from the tribal past, runic meanings should be explored in contemporary terms. However, the function of this book is to explore the oldest possible meanings.

I would also like to stress here that although I have researched the runic lore to explore the

Germanic origins of the symbols, I in no way support any form of right-wing nationalism. Nazis stole and misappropriated many runic symbols, following the misguided Aryan creeds of the late 1800s. Not only were many of the runes used out of context, but they also promoted a version of the past that never actually happened. There is no such thing as 'purity of race' anywhere.

Please note that I use the Norse term, Kenning, often. A kenning is not only a simile, but is often part riddle. The rune poems are full of them.

Many thanks for purchasing this wee book.

Dave Migman, Stone Mad Crafts

Abbreviations used:

OERP - Old English Rune Poem
ONRP - Old Norwegian Rune Poem
OIRP - Old Icelandic Rune Poem
PIE - Proto-Indo-European
IE - Indo-European
AS - Anglo Saxon
OI - Old Irish
ON - Old Norse

OE   - Old English

Sources: the rune poems

The majority of our modern information concerning the runes comes from scant literary sources. These are the following: The Old English Rune Poem (OERP), The Old Norwegian Rune Poem (ONRP), The Old Icelandic Rune Poem (OIRP). There is also the Abecedarium Nordmannicum, which is little more than a list to recall runic order. Added to this are literary sources and references to the runes such as the Hávamál (Sayings Of The High-One) and Sigrdrífumál (The Lay of Sigurd).

The Old English Rune Poem

The Old English Rune Poem is known from copies made from an older medieval manuscript, which was lost in a fire in 1731. The poem catalogues the twenty-four original *futhark* runes in the language of the West Saxons. This alphabet was known to the Saxons as *Futhorc*. There are also add-ons, or modern runes, which evolved as Anglo-Saxon language developed (I have not included these and concentrate solely on the original twenty-four). The poem itself may date from the early tenth century in origin - however, some scholars contend this date and argue a much earlier origin. As with the ONRP, the scribe flavours the text with the religion of his time. It is the earliest and most extensive of the rune poems.

The Old Norwegian Rune Poem

The Old Norwegian Rune Poem exists as a medieval manuscript, dated from the Thirteenth

Century. This copy was destroyed by fire in 1728 (three years before the OERP was destroyed). However translations have been made from seventeenth century copies. In this poem the scribe infused his Christian creed onto the template, or word hoard, that he worked from. Obviously working from a store house of traditional themes, he appears to have superimposed the ethics of his times onto the root of some of the symbols, especially in the central section, *Hagal's ætt*. Only the sixteen younger *futhark* are described.

The Old Icelandic Rune Poem

The earliest facsimile of the *Old Icelandic Rune Poem* is dated to the fifteenth century and is much damaged. Some elements can be discerned by comparing later medieval and seventeenth century manuscripts. Of course this invites disagreements in translations. The poem uses a consistent method of three 'kennings' for each symbol. The poem lists the sixteen characters of the younger *Futhark*, which is the later, condensed version of the runic alphabet.

Abecedarium Nordmannicum

Abecedarium Nordmannicum is sometimes listed as a runic source, but appears to be little more than an aid to strengthen memory.

The origins of the runic alphabet

The use of runes spans many centuries. In fact the earliest recorded finds are from 1st c. A.D., while runes were still being used, mingled with sigils and other occult images during the 1800s in Iceland (eg Galdabok). As the plethora of rune casting books out there testify, they are still much in use today.

In ancient times they were used in a variety of practices. A *Hellirûnâro* was a male necromancer, while a *Tôtrûna* (death-runer) was a female necromancer, they used *hellirûnas* (Hell-runes) for their magic. Similarily *Haliurunnae* (Hell-runer) was the ancient Gothic word for a sorceress, *rûnokarl* (rune-man) a magician. In fact there are traces of the word throughout the ancient Germanic and Scandinavian world. The German word for Mandrake still retains its ancient form, *Alraun* (Great Rune), hinting at its magical properties.

The association of necromantic cults with Odin is also an interesting development. In the West, 2000 years of Christianity led to a polarisation of good and evil, which the 'enlightenment' never managed to assuage, only absorbed within humanist projects. However the boundaries of what was evil or good were more amorphous in pre-Christian times. *Odin*, the All-father, was a god of poetry but he also had dealings with the slain. It was said that he could converse with the dead, and was also known as the *god of the gallows*. We must remember that death was not something that was hidden away, but very prevalent in people's lives in such times. Bodies were thought to be embarking upon a journey, hence the predilection for boat burning funeral pyres and boat shaped graves. This imagery is profoundly poetic and ancient. It is a seed in Bronze-age Indo-European thought, glimpsed in archaeological finds of birdprowed boats with solar sails. The notion of the sun descending into the underworld is important in mythology; traceable in the ancient funerary practices of northern Europe and further afield - such as the sun barge of Ra, the Egyptian sun god.

Though runes were often evident in the mundane and everyday, they were used magically too. It may be that inscribing runic symbols on items was accompanied with magical songs. Chants and songs have long been seen as magical in many cultures across the world. *'Roner'* were magical spells, recorded in Danish folk songs, while, in Finland, the word rune was probably originally connected with magical songs. In many Icelandic and Scandinavian sagas, runes are referred to in a magical context.

Runes could be written backwards, from right to left or vice-versa. Sometimes they appear without punctuation, and symbols were often repeated for emphasis. Inscriptions could also run in rows like a ploughed field, or flow along serpentine forms. Letters could also be combined to form bind-runes and symbols, such as pine tree emblems and Swastikas, which also appear alongside inscriptions (especially the bracteate medallions of the Germanic sphere). Runes appeared on a variety of materials, wood, bone, metals, stone and a variety of objects too.

Shaved off were the runes - that of old were written,
And mixed with the holy mead,
And sent on ways so wide;
So the gods had them - so the elves got them,
And some for the Wanes so wise,
And some for mortal men.

(*Sigrdrífumál* - Henry Bellow trans.)

Etymological origins of the word 'rune' often involve secrets, knowledge, mystery and counsel. Here are some examples:

Old Irish, *rún* = hidden, occult, mystery, thoughts, knowledge.
Medieval Welsh, *rhin* = intimate mystery, or something private.
Gothic, *garūni* = counsel, consultation.
Old English, ryn = Symbol & *geryne* = mystery, secret, symbol.
Saxon, *girūni* = mystery.

Proponents of the reconstructed Indo-European language might point to the root of these as held in common, **reu-* (howl or bellow). Latin *'rumour'* (hearsay) also shares a common root, but refers to the 'talk of many', equating the murmur of a stream with people. However some refute the IE theory, and prefer to draw the origin of 'rune' from Greek, ἐρέω, ἐρέομαι, (to ask or enquire).

The argument for who loaned 'rune' as a word, Celt or German, appears to swing back and forth. The fact is that both cultures encountered each other on the continent, warred and traded and obviously exchanged religio-cultural spheres of interest (both stemming from IE origins). This is blazingly obvious in the parallels which two of their major deities, *Woden* and *Lug* possessed.

The first runic inscription has been dated from the first century AD and it was used throughout Germanic Europe for a millennia. With the migrations of many Germanic tribes in the 4th Century AD, usage spread.

Samples can be found as far away as Portugal. Ironically the second generation Norsemen who settled in the north of France, the Normans (Northmen), were responsible for the decline of runic use in Britain. However it had pretty much faded from use on the continent by then in favour of the language of the ecclesiastical establishment, Latin.

*Camunic from the 4th -3rd Centuries BC
is an Etruscan language.*

a b g d e v z h g i k l m
n ś o p ś q r s t u ϕ χ ψ ? ?

Eldar Futhark alphabet

f u th a r k g w h i n j ï p s z
t b e m l ng d o

Of the origins of the runes there are many theories. Most focus around the thought that runes evolved from similar scripts of Latin, Greek or

Etruscan origin. As you can see in the diagram there are some similar looking symbols, even if their sounds appear different. Then there is the mythological tale, of how the all-father, Odin, discovered the runes. This story is most interesting and will be explored further later on. There is a very strong case that Germanic usage lies in offsprings of Etruscan alphabets such as the *Rhaetic* language and *Camunic*. *Raetia* was a region roughly covering modern Southern Germany, north of the Alps. The *Rhaetians* were displaced from the Po valley region of Italy when earlier Celtic migrations intruded upon their territory. Archaeological finds have unearthed numerous inscribed offerings from temples to *Reita* (also known as *Artemis Orthia*). Some of these use the word ALU, which also appears in early Germanic runic inscriptions.

Reita was an ancient goddess of writing and letters, dating from the 4-5th Century BC. Her places of worship are often located near healing wells or springs. She appears to also have had links with the underworld/otherworld. She was a popular goddess and shrines appear in the lands of the *Veneti* (another tribe using a script developed from Etruscan), and her temples also spread as far as Austria. *Artemis Orthia's** origins lay in the land of the Spartans and may have reached northern Italy and the lands of the Rhaetians via trade routes across the Adriatic. The oldest dedication to *Reita* was found on a pair of greaves found at Pergine, dated to the 10th Century BC.

Whatever its origins, Runic usage began while the Roman Empire was still flourishing. Germanic warriors often enlisted as mercenaries in the Legions, fighting across the Empire. However as Imperial Rome began to fall apart, Germanic tribes began to push into their territory. The Germanic migrations began in the 4th Century and lasted until the 6th. Tribes from the Eastern steppes, such as the Huns, had been pushing into tribal territory and a movement of peoples began. Goths, Vandals, Visigoths and Lombards pushed into other territories across Europe.

Bracteate are gold medallions used as talismans and they date from this period. The bracteate form a large corpus of runic finds. These gold coins date from 300-600 A.D. and though samples are found in Britain, finds are condensed around Denmark, Jutland, Sweden and Germany. Their origins point to close Roman influences. However rather than copies of Roman coins they adopt a Germanic style of their own. These medallions may point to the rise of an elite, possibly warriors returning from duties and service in the Roman army. Their usage appears to be both magical and socio-political. There is evidence to suggest some designs may refer to the idea of an *ideal king*. Germanic/Norse mythology can be clearly seen on other bracteate, such as images of *Tyr* with his hand in Fenrir's mouth, or images of Odin. A symbolic combination of symbol and image is evidently at play in many of these images on the bracteate.

The 2nd Century saw an increase in the usage of runes across the Germanic world. They found their way into the Scandinavian world and the Anglo Saxons brought them to Britain. Thus runic alphabets diverge, mutate and evolve, often reflecting changes in language. This is reflected in the rune poems, which do not always see eye-to-eye.

We have to remember that the OERP and others are products of their time. Christianity was the norm across much of Europe, and the scribes tended to work in monastic outposts, and therefore were Christian. For example, the Ruthwell cross, in Dumfriesshire, is Christian in content -

reciting the poem called *The Rood*, which tells the passion of Christ from the cross' viewpoint. However in the lands of the AS, runes appear to have kept a tenacious place, despite the Latin script being available and popular from the 7th Century onwards. *Runology* was an interest reserved mostly for scholars, both secular and religious, and often used in cryptographic alphabets, to encode messages through texts. Their use in England lasted until the 11th Century, most likely because the Church adopted the runic system, albeit altering it - this is why runes appear in religious works from the Anglo Saxon kingdom of Northumbria. The Frank's Caskets, a carved ivory casket, is a stunning example adorned with scenes described in OE runes. A telling mix of Christian and Pagan myth.

In fact the legacy of AS runic use is still reflected in modern English to this day with the Germanic verbs: **wrītan* was to cut the runes, which became '*to write*'. While **rēðan*, to interpret the runes, became '*to read*'.

On the continent, the end of the Elder Futhark and the rise of its condensed, younger version of 16 rows, is dated to approximately the 8th Century. The Younger Futhark retained its three rows, but had six in its first row and five in the other two. Though the use of runes continued prolifically in Scandinavia, its use on the continent declined with the advent of Christianity and the use of Latin. In England, the AS runes were adopted by the clergy, 'reformed', and put to use for ecclesiastical purposes. It appears their use in a pagan sense went out of vogue and as the medieval period ensued, the runes diverged greatly from their original meanings, even when used magically. A sort of demonised version begins, in which *Odin* and *Thor's* names are mentioned alongside Satan and other hellish demons.

Runic research begins in the 15th Century, but the first real, scholarly work is by Ole Worm, in 1651, in his tome, *Danica Literatura Antiquissima*,

Vulgo Gothica Dicta. He decided the runes predated Greek and Latin and their name meant 'cut' or 'groove'. In the 19th Century, Runic studies were undertaken once again by men of learning. A thesis was proposed in which Denmark, Scandinavia and Britain were one vast kingdom, ruled by Dacians, Goths and Vandals. This empire was termed the *Runick Kingdom* and the inhabitants were *Runians*. Modern academia is just as susceptible to trends and fashions, the current being the widespread disregard for runes as magical, when all evidence points to the contrary. However, it does appear that magical use declined as the population became more literate in runic. Archaeological discoveries from Bergen in 1955 revealed that as more people became versed in the Futhark alphabet, their use as symbols of power decreased. Finds of rune staves, or *rúnakefli*, reveal mainly mundane use of runes, such as communication between merchants, lovers, etc.

*

Artemis Orthia - the second name means

'wordy'.

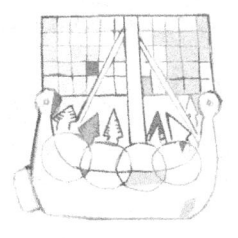

Runes and their use in magic

"auspicia sortesque ut qui maxime observant. sortium consuetudo simplex. virgam frugiferae arbori decisam in surculos amputant eosque notis quibusdam discretos super candidam vestam temere ac fortuito spargunt. mox, si publice consultatur, sacerdos civitatis, sin privatim, ipse pater familiae, precatus deos caelumque suspiciens, ter singulos tollit, sublatos secundum impressam ante notam interpretatur."

"For omens and the casting of lots they have the highest regard. Their procedure in casting lots is always the same. They cut off a branch of a nut-bearing tree and slice it into strips; these they mark with different signs and throw them completely at random onto a white cloth. Then the priest of state, if the consultation is a public one, or the father of the family if it is private, offers a prayer to the gods, and looking up at the sky picks up three strips, one at a time, and reads their meaning from the signs previously scored on them."

(Tacitus, *Germania*, Chpt 10)

This was recorded by Tacitus in the first century AD. It has been debated whether he was recording an actual casting of runes or some other form of divination. The description certainly evokes the runes. He refers to the symbol adorned strips as notis, (plural of nota). Scholars, comparing the use of this word with other contemporary writers such as Cicero, conclude that Notis is a reference to runes. So this would seem to be a direct, eye witness account of a rune casting.

However rune-craft wasn't solely confined to the realm of augury. The corpus of early Germanic finds, dating from the 1st - 6th Century AD reveals many inscriptions that can only be described as magical in intent. There are also ample examples of runic charms, some which follow certain patterns or sequences. For example, an Icelandic Charm reads; 'I carve for you eight *æsir*, nine needs'. The latter referring to *nauthiz/nauth*, while the *Aesir* rune is *ansuz/óss*, that is *Odin's* symbol, god. This repeated eight times hints at the three families of the Futhark and enforces the power of the numbers. The repeating of '*ása átta*', each a-rune perhaps representing major deities in a pantheon of Germanic deities, must have been a powerful symbol.

In finds from Denmark/Sweden, Gotland and Frisia, dated to between 300A.D. - 600A.D. we find the use of a crossed bind rune, combining *Gebo* (g), with *Ansuz* (a). This rune is repeated thrice, yielding *gagaga*. We do not know if sound also played a part, and if these charms were read aloud. One school of thought suggests that the OERP was meant to be sung. According to the *Hávamál*, speaking, knowing and carving played an integral part in magical rites. In many forms of magic, repetition reinforces power. This, combined with certain numerological formulae, eg; sets of three, sets of eight and nine, all reference Germanic and Norse myth. There are sacred triads of gods and goddesses, there are eight runes in three sets, and there are nine-worlds etc. Such repetition appears in Iceland during the late 1600's, documented in a curious collection of sigils and runic inscriptions.

The *Galdrabók* is a mash of Christian occultism and bastardised fragments of older lore. There are here mentioned 'fart-runes' enabled through the formulae of 'eight a-runes, nine n-runes, thirteen þ-runes' (Otte ausse Naudir Nije þossa ðretten), written in blood upon calf's skin. The subject would become immobilised by endless farts.

Fart runes from the 1600s.

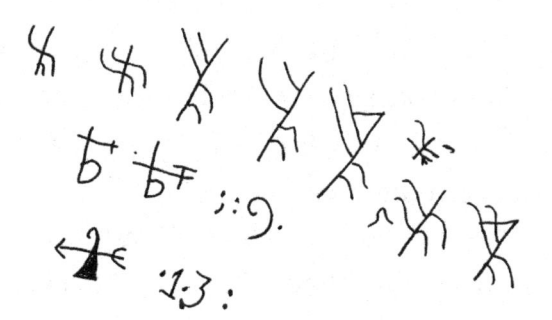

It is obvious from the wealth of archaeological evidence that runic inscriptions on artefacts, talismans and monumental stones existed

for various purposes. Discounting the mundane, and funerary inscriptions, there is ample evidence to point to their use in magic.

Bracteate fascinate me. As mentioned in the previous chapter, these golden medallions were used as talismans. They were influenced by Roman coins, and early samples are almost facsimiles, however pretty quickly a Germanic animal style begins to dominate. Images that are mythic, cultic and possibly political adorn these medallions (they were worn, and not used as currency). The runic inscriptions are varied. Symbols such as pine trees and swastikas appear amongst cryptic runic inscriptions and occasional Roman numerals. Certain words are found on many items, the main being: ALU, LAUKAZ, AUJA, which are all interesting in their own right.

Alu may well be the *Ol-Runar*, or the Ale-runes that the Valkyrie, *Sigrdrifar* reveals to the hero, *Sigurdr* in the poem *Sigrdrífumál*. The direct translation of ALU is Ale, and this may hint at rituals in which beer was used to alter the state of consciousness. Others translate ALU as meaning 'dedication', a sort of 'hail by ale'. It seems apparent that the act of including this word was significant. It could also be that each rune was viewed in its own right, *ansuz+ laguz + uruz*, the combination of this triad then being seen as potent, with the meaning of the word itself adding another layer of symbolic interpretation to the sequence.

Auja is a protective sequence, and translates as fortune and luck. A preoccupation with destiny and fate were integral to Germanic life. In the Germanic concept of cosmology, the *Nornir* were the three fates of past, present and future. They sometimes drew lots (runes) or wove a tapestry of fate, each thread a single life, ending when cut. They worked their loom, each fingernail painted with a rune. The same myth persisted in Pagan Scandinavia with the three *Norns. Laukaz* means leek. Leeks were magical and phallic symbols, and concepts such as sexuality and fertility were implied by its use.

A common formulae in runic tradition was to state the name of the creator/carver, eg; X made me, and sometimes the whole Futhark alphabet was inscribed in sequence. This might have been a teaching aid, or simply a magical formulae, invoking the power of each symbol. Some references even appear to be kennings for *Woden*, such as:

'The one with the gleaming eye consecrated these runes'.

It is told in the verses of the *Hávamál* (The Sayings of the High One) how *Odin* hung from the great boughs of the world tree, *Yggdrasil*, for nine nights. Hanging appears to have been a way to ritually sacrifice to the All-father. A 19th Century song from the Shetlands contains echos of this.

> *'Nine days he hung fa de rutless tree...*
> *A bloo bluidy maet wis in his side,...*
> *Nine lang nachts I'da nippin' rime.'*

In this state *Odin* reached through the boundary between worlds and the runes were revealed to him. A detailed version is given within the Poetic Edda, the poem, *Hávamál*. The latter portion of this skald is filled with powerful, ritualistic overtones of death and resurrection. The imagery is extremely evocative of 'shamanic', practices (even though the term is not without its problems, I use it here for convenience sake).

> *Them Hropt arranged, and them he wrote,*
> *And them in thought he made,*

*Out of the draught that down had dropped
From the head of Heithdraupnir,
And the horn of Hoddrofnir.*

*On the mountain he stood with Brimir's sword,
On his head the helm he bore;
Then first the head of Mimir spoke forth,
And words of truth it told.*

Hropt is one of *Odin's* many names. *Heithdraupnir* (light-dropper) and *Hoddrofnir* (Treasure opener) are 'kennings' for *Mimir*. Often likened to a giant, *Mimir* is one of the *Aesir*. *Yggdrasil* means *Odin's Steed* but it was also known as *Mimameidr*, *Mimir's* Tree. Deep beneath the tree, under one of *Yggdrasil's* roots, near the land of the Frost giants was *Mimisbrunn, Mimir's* well. Here all true knowledge and understanding bubbled up.

Odin acquired great knowledge from *Mimir*, but myths vary. Thus we have the tale of how *Odin* took *Mimir's* head after he was decapitated by the *Vanir*. As Snorre Sturlusson tells us in the *Ynglinga* Saga:

"... then the Vanir suspected that the Æsir had cheated them in the exchange of men. Then they took Mímir and decapitated him and sent the head to the Æsir.

Óðinn took the head and smeared it with herbs that prevented it from decaying, and spoke spells over it and enchanted it so that it spoke to him and told him many secret things."

The Eddic Poem, The *Völuspá* (47), even mentions *Odin's* taking counsel from *Mimir's* head.

*Yggdrasil shakes, and shiver on high
The ancient limbs, and the giant is loose;
To the head of Mim does Odin give heed,
But the kinsman of Surt shall slay him soon.*

This idea of a decapitated head possessing great knowledge is mirrored in ancient Celtic myths. In one such tale the Head of the mighty hero, *Finn* is preserved after being lopped off. During a subsequent feast *Finn's* head demands his '*mir*', or portion, from those gathered in the same house, before reciting his songs. Many other stories of severed heads echo *Odin's* use of *Mimir's* head. These heads are usually associated with poetry and wisdom. Celtic headhunting and the cult of the severed head attests to this idea. Heads were seen as sacred, the place where the soul resided. Celtic myth also abounds with tales of speaking heads, filled with knowledge and poetry.

Given that *Mimir's* name stems from IE, **(s)mer-*, which means to remember, we can see the importance of this theme. In times where oral traditions were prevalent, the capacity of retaining knowledge was all important.

There are parallels in myths of other cultures too. In Hades, by *Mnemosyne's Well*, the dead would prepare for the onward journey into the realm of the dead. The well was situated to the right of the entry to the underworld, and a white cypress grew beside it. In Norse myth the *Norns* plastered white mud on the trunk of the world tree. In Ireland the myth is mirrored in the legend of the *Boand*, the spirit of the River Boyne. She was one of the divine race known as the *Tuatha De Danann*. She went searching for the *Well of Segais*, a well of knowledge that lay at the source of the Boyne. Carelessly she walked thrice around the well anti-clockwise, angering the well. Three waves lashed at her, taking her eye and disfiguring her hand and foot. This parallels Norse tales in which *Odin* pledged an eye for a sup from *Mimir's* well.

Such links with Greek or Celtic legends point to an innate human understanding. The familiarity of certain concepts and symbols, are lodged deep within our collective conscious. If we were to separate each thread from the myth, each legendary component into some form of codified stratagem, we can create a psychological map for the modern to relate to. *Mimir* is a giant concept, a well that *Odin*, in his search for knowledge, taps into. Knowledge and understanding are immense in their breadth and their depth. Too much knowledge can turn a man blind too, for not all knowledge is 'good', and insight can be hard earned. The German Philosopher, Frederick Nietzsche's allusion to the abyss is relevant here - *and if thou gaze long into an abyss, the abyss will also gaze into thee.* The well has depths for a purpose and every shaman's journey contains an element of danger. The essence of *Mimir* is the keystone to the runic lore - for it is *Mimir*, the very stuff of prime knowledge, that reveals the runes to *Odin*. *Mimir* is neither person nor well, but that which is contained within.

As well as the *Hávamál, Sigrdrífumál* is an important text for runic information. It lists types of runes and is quite specific. *Tyr* is mentioned as a victory-rune as are ale-runes, speech and mind-runes etc. Where possible, I have added verses from this intriguing poem where I think they bear relevance. I will included the relevant sections of the poem in the appendix.

There were obviously rites and rituals concerning the inscribing and using of runes. In the *Hávamál* the narrator's voice rises from the text to quiz the reader, laying out a structure to runic implementation. Writing, Interpreting, colouring, testing, asking, offering, sending and sacrificing.

He bade write on the shield before the shining goddess
on Arvak's ear and on Alsvith's hoof
on the wheel of a car of Hrungnir's killer
on Slepnir's teeth and the straps of the sledge
On the paws of the bear and on Bragi's tongue
on the wolf's claws bared
and the eagle's beak
on bloody wings, and bridge's end

on freeing hands and helping foot-prints
On glass and on gold, and on goodly charms
In wine and in beer and on well loved seats
On Grungir's point and Grani's breast
on the nails of Norns and the night Owl's beak!

(*Sigrdrifumal*, Verses 16 -17, Trans. Bellows)

The Ættir

I am One who becomes Two,
Who becomes Four,
Who becomes Eight,
and then I am One again.

(Ancient Egyptian funerary text)

The Greeks split their alphabet into three groups of eight, as did the Germanic tribes with futhark. These they called ætt or ættir , which means family. The ætts are named Frey's family, Hagal's Family and Tyr's family. The prevalence of the number eight in Germanic and Norse cosmology* is interesting and draws parallels with other I.E. cultures. Eight is the Egyptian God, Thoth's number, and he is the Egyptian god of writing, poetry and eloquence.

He is a psychopomp, and negotiates the realm between mortals and gods. In Greece the same god was named Hermes, interchangeable with the Roman Mercury. In The Gallic Wars, Julius Caesar wrote that the chief god of the Celts was Mercury. This deity was known to the Celts as Lug, the god of all crafts. He shared many qualities with the Germanic god Woden. They held many things in common, Woden and Lug were armed with great spears and their favoured modes of transport were mythic steeds that could navigate between worlds. Both are associated with ravens that brought them news of events from afar. The Roman writer, Tacitus, also says of the Germanic tribes that their main god is Mercurius. It is interesting to note that many tales of Odin (and Odr) relate that he travelled far and wide and was known by many different names. Perhaps this reflects the recognition that many deities had similarities.

Egyptians and other cultures, such as Greek, held mystery traditions involving their alphabets. There is a case to be made for the continuation of such notions. Cultures readily exchanged ideas as they traded and settled. As I detailed in the previous chapter, the runic alphabet appears to have developed in *Raetia*, possibly transferred along the Rhine by artisans, or Germanic mercenaries who had fought for the Romans and were stationed in that land. The splitting of the runes into three ætts may mirror *Rhaetic* inscriptions to the goddess *Reita*, in which the alphabet is split into three parts. However it is interesting to note here that in the Germanic and Norse cosmology, the *Nornir*, three giantesses who laboured around the well of *Urd*, weave the tapestry of fate. They were Urð (fate), Verðandi (being) and Skuld (what is owed). These can be interpreted as past, present and future. Each had a rune on each fingernail. Here we have a possible mythic explanation for the splitting of the Futhark into three groups. The symbolic reference of past, present and future. Could it be, that in drawing lots, the *ættir* could also be so grouped? Even in cartomancy to this day a standard, three-card draw follows this sequence.

It is interesting to note that in myth, *Frey*, *Odin* and *Tyr* form a triumvirate. In the runes we appear to possess remnants of this, with the obvious occlusion of *Odin*. Could it be that originally the middle set belonged to *Odin*? Perhaps the other deities were deemed less threatening than

Woden to the early ecclesiastical establishment, and therefore his name was dropped, whilst theirs remained. It is interesting to note that in the ONRP, the second *ætt* appears more 'Christianised' than the others, with subtle references to Christian values, such as charity, poverty and the necessity to lead 'the blind' (heathens). There is also the final rune of the set, *Sowilo*, the sun, compared to the Almighty. However in Scandinavian and Germanic myth, the Sun was a female deity, which points to the inference of Christianity assigning the sun as a symbol for their god. Taking these things into consideration; that the middle *ætt* in the ONRP is the most heavily Christianised section, this could be evidence of the scribe over-compensating to rid this family of, what may have been, overtly pagan overtones. It would make sense to assume that Christians adapted the poems over time to suit their own agenda. It was after all Church policy to assimilate the ancient creeds, or that which belonged to them, and subvert it over time. This is plainly evident when reading the rune poems.

My theory is that much that reeked of heathenism was altered and tamed by the scribes. However, that which was deemed less of a threat was assimilated, perhaps because deities had been downgraded to heroes, or simply forgotten (see *Mannaz* and *Ingwaz*). In the Eddas of Snorre Sturlusson there is a conscious effort to historicise mythology. Therefore Odin and the *Asa* come from Troy (many cultures thought it prudent to trace their descent to the fabled city) and Snorre tells us that the *Asa* came from Asia (his theory being the word *Aesir* was related to Asia - an etymologically incorrect assumption). Historical characters such as Attila the Hun appear in Snorre's Eddas and are woven into the myths. This can be seen as a need to explain the remnant folklore and deities to the Christian world. In their world view there could only be one ultimate god. It was not that Christianity said that such things didn't exist, but that the old gods and goddesses were either demonised or made into old kings and queens. Here Snorri, in an attempt worthy of later rationalists, attempts to explain the gods in an historical way.

What has been lost? Much I think. What was *Ingwaz* to the ancient Germanic practitioners of rune-craft? Surely it must have held a different meaning to later Christianised practitioners. Laying the runes out in sequence gives me the strong impression that there is some process behind their configuration. I have wondered if the eight runes in the three sets were actually arranged as masculine and feminine pairs. However some of the names are neutral too. But there appears to be obvious significance in their arrangement. Symbolic interplay is evident between symbols as they arranged in each family. For instance, *Feoh*: cattle are domesticated, tame. They are steered and guided and a source of wealth. They benefit the community to which they belong, through meat, milk, skins and trade. The following rune is another bovine. *Uruz*, auroch, undomesticated, wild, unpredictable. A beast that was held and awe, feared, hunted and fought, but respected. It appears to be no accident that these runes are neighbours.

*Of course other numbers predominate Norse myth too, Three and Nine especially.

STONE MAD RUNES

The Futhark

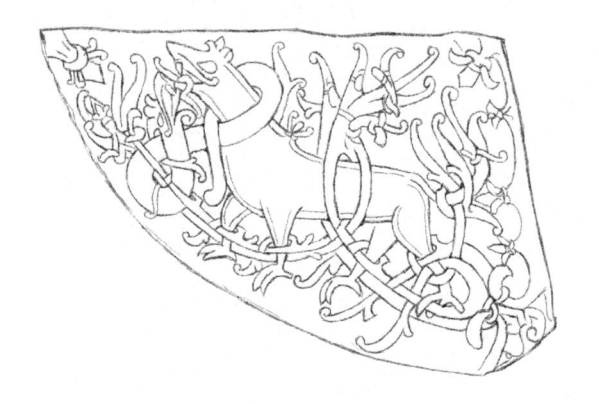

Here are all twenty-four original runes.

Freyr's ætt

Fé/ Feoh

OERP

(feoh) byþ frōfur fīra gehwylcum;
sceal ðēah manna gehwylc miclun hyt dǣlan,
gif hē wile for Drihtne dōmes hlēotan.

Wealth is welcome for all men
Yet each must share it freely
If he wants to earn
Glory before the lord

OIRP

f er frænda róg, ok fyrða gaman, ok grafseiðs gata.

f is family strife, and men's delight, and grave-fish's path (serpent).

ONRP

Fé vældr frænda róge; foðesk ulfr í skóge.

Wealth causes family strife; the wolf is reared/ feeds in the forest.

T he first rune of Freyr's family, it lords over the rest. It means wealth, specifically cattle - that being the prime source of tribal wealth, and hence the connotation of this symbol with 'transitory wealth'. Freyr is also known as the giver of cattle, fégjafi. Indeed the symbol itself may be a pictogram of the profile of a bull.

This was a fortunate rune for a lot cast. In tribal societies, wealth shared benefitted the whole community. Numerous examples are to be found in literature, such as the epic *Beowulf*, in which the giving of gifts, such as silver rings, was honoured. Sharing wealth promoted mutual respect and honour, bonding giver and receiver. Important alliances were forged this way. It refers also to the honour involved in such endeavours.

In the OERP the overtones of a tribal, warrior society are explicit. In context, *Feoh* applies to all moveable wealth, and in the warrior's case, as demonstrated by the epic, *Beowulf*, this can mean the sword, or spear, a warrior carried and the armour that protected them. It reflects a positive sense of honour, between clansmen, between bands and families. Gifts were also used in marriage ceremonies, such the ring exchanging ceremonies still used today.

Feoh also confers a warning. Wealth can also inflame jealousy if coveted. This points to an awareness of managing material goods. Cattle, being the embodiment of wealth in bygone eras, indicate that this is not necessarily a reference to money. But *Feoh's* material groundings imply that this was not a reference to spiritual wealth, despite some modern interpretations.

There are parallels in Norse myth. The Serpent's way, mentioned in the OIRP, may be a reference to the Dragon's hoard in the Volsung saga. *Fafnir*, the dragon, warns *Sigurdr* of the price of his treasure. Indeed the warrior does not share the wealth and, once he slays the dragon, he is corrupted by it. This has a knock-on effect. The malignancy of greed and the bad luck brought by his actions ruins his family.

In the ONRP, the allusion to wolves is made. The wolf feeds/is reared alone in the forest. Despite the reality of nature, wolves, in most northern myths, represent malignant forces. Here it refers to the negative connotations of *Feoh's* wealth. Poetically we can visualise the rage of jealously that rattles the bars of its cage (the tree trunks). Wolves were also associated with outlaws. To become 'outlaw' was to be banished from society. A crushing punishment in a harsh world; to be denied the bonds tribal society afforded. The wolf that howls in the forest echoes this state: The outlaw in the wild, shunned and despised.

Unfortunately for wolves, Norse myth held them in disdain much of the time. Though respected for their ferocity by warriors, wishing to emulate their fierceness, wolves get a bad rap. *Fenris/Fenrir* is the great wolf of winter, destined to swallow the sun. He is ever *Odin's* eternal enemy, and it is against Fenrir's forces that *Odin* marshals the *Einherjar*. The heroes of past battles are assembled in *Valhöl*, awaiting the final battle of *Ragnorak*, a battle that will see *Odin* consumed by the terrible wolf. The presence of the wolf as an individual serves to warn against the loss of community values - giving balance to this symbol.

Reference:

The Norwegian Rune Poem in context: Style, Structure & Imagery - Veronka Szöke

The Rune Primer - Sweyn Plowright

Rudiments of Runelore - Stephen Pollington

The Old English Rune Poem - A critical Edition - Maureen Halsall

Runic & Hero Poems of the Old Teutonic Peoples - edited by Bruce Dickins

Uruz/Ur

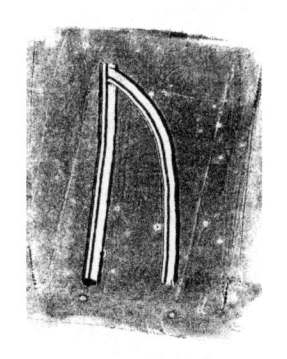

OERP

(ūr) byþ anmōd and oferhyrned,
felafrēcne dēor - feohteþ mid hornum
- mre mōrstapa; þæt is mōdig wuht!

Aurochs are fierce and high-horned
the courageous beast fights with its horns
a well-known moor-treader
it is a brave creature

OIRP

U er skyja grátr, ok skára þverrir, ok hirðis hatr.

Drizzle is the cloud's tears
and the harvest's ruin
and the herder's hate

ONRP

Úr er af illu jarne, opt løypr ræinn á hjarne.

Slag is from bad iron, oft lopes the reindeer over the frozen snow.

After the herd comes the raging beast. This is the massive Auroch, standing almost two metres tall at the shoulder. A solid slab of a thing, muscles rippling, steam rising from its scarred flanks, and its long, skewering horns, like massive spear tips. Unfortunately, this impressive creature has been extinct since the 1600s. Aurochs were long vanished from Norway, Iceland and Britain by the time the respective rune poems were transcribed as we know them now. It appears that the symbol was transformed, retaining the imagery of strength, but replaced with the image of the smith at his forge, as reflected in the kennings of the OIRP & ONRP. These could also simple refer to weather, storms and tempests. The OERP retains the original meaning of this rune. However, the others, in referring to its meaning as slag and drizzle, might be alluding to sparks from a forge. Here, there may also be an allusion to Weland/Volundr, the mythical smith. It is likely that the drizzle reference exists because ON úr (slag) is a homonym of OE uruz (auroch). Due to the Auroch's decline and scarcity it is likely that this replaced the original meaning. Aurochs just weren't relevant anymore, but drizzle is never in short supply.

The Auroch version remains closer to the original meaning, and a testament to the power of this fearsome beast of the woods, that it retained its form in the OERP. However, the primal Auroch was not a 'moor stalker', it inhabited forests. Tacitus informs us that Aurochs were prized by Germanic tribesmen. Hunting one was seen as a rite of passage. Auroch horns were lined with silver and used at feasts. They were highly prized possessions.

Perhaps the power of the beast can be glimpsed on the base plate of the Gundestrup cauldron. This magnificent silver cauldron is dated between the 1st - 2nd Centuries B.C. It was found in a bog in Jutland. It consists of silver plates, five interior and seven exterior, which depict various mythological scenes. The origins are attributed to a Celtic tribe who commissioned the piece from Thracian silversmiths and then it was subsequently carried off north in a raid. The base-plate reveals a ritualistic scene involving an Auroch, which rises from the base and dominates the scene. Here we can sense the true potency of this monster. In this scene the Auroch is passive, and has been killed, or is dying, either in hunt or sacrifice, yet it dwarfs the other figures.

Here we have the venerated and feared moor-stalker. In referencing the moor, a wild place is summoned, a place that filled people with unease - untamed, mysterious and magical. Perhaps it is where ancient, half-remembered gods and goddesses inhabited. In *Beowulf*, the murderous Grendel is also referred to in this same manner, *mōrstapa* - 'moor-stalker'.

Symbolically, *Uruz* functions on different levels. One is to denote strength, courage and stamina, but it also warns of such a beast as an obstacle, something otherworldly and unseen, ferocious and waiting. It forms an opposite to the tame cattle in *Feoh*, for the Auroch is something wild, unexpected, a challenge and a danger.

Reference:

Names of the u-Rune - Futhark Runic Studies vol 1 (2010) - Inmaculada Senra Silva

The Norwegian Rune Poem in context: Style, Structure and Imagery - Veronka Szöke

The Old English Rune Poem - A critical Edition - Maureen Halsall

An Encyclopaedia of the Barbarian world Vol 1 (8000B.C - 1000 A.D) - Peter Bogucki & Pam J. Crabtree (Editors)

An Archaeology of Images - Miranda Alehouse

DAVE MIGMAN

Green

Runic & Hero Poems of the Old Teutonic Peoples - edited by Bruce Dickins

þurisaz/ ðorn

OERP

*(ðorn) byþ ðearle scearp, ðegna gehwylcum
anfengys yfyl, ungemetun rēþe
manna gehwylcun ðe him mid resteð.*

Thorn is painfully sharp to any warrior
seizing it is bad,
excessively severe
for any person who lays among them

OIRP

Þ er kvenna kvol, ok kletta ibūi, ok Valrúnar verr.

Thurs is women's illness
and a cliff-dweller
and the victory rune man/husband

ONRP

Þurs vældr kvinna kvillu, kátr værðr fár af illu.

Giant's cause women' disorder
few are made happy by anger.

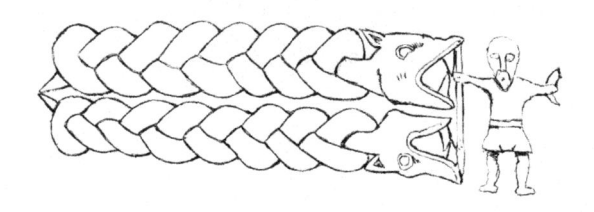

Perhaps in this rune, we have the conscious effort of the Anglo-Saxon scribe to eliminate traces of the heathen god, Thor. In the OERP Thorn becomes exactly that, the spiny tree. The warning is implicit, and so why would warriors grasp at thorns? And who would lay amongst them? There are early medieval accounts of sacrifices in which victims endured a death by thorn bushes. It might be that such sacrifices were made to Thor and that the warrior reference reflects Thor's belligerence. Nonetheless, hard Thorns protect tender fruit, and this protective quality is engendered by the rune.

OERP may also refer obliquely to *Thorn* as a sleep charm, as mentioned in *Sigrdrífumál*, when the Valkyrie, *Sigrdrifá* tells the hero, *Sigurdr*, that *Odin* 'pricked her with a sleep-thorn' because she brought down a warrior he favoured.

In the OIRP & ONRP the subject, *Thurs*, is described as a dweller of cliffs, crags and mountains. This location is true of thorny trees and bushes. However, these are also the haunts of thunder gods such as *Thunor/Thor/Perun* and his archetypal ilk. The later viking legends are full of tales of *Thor's* victories over giants, and he is quite fond of battling giantesses too. Giantesses were associated with elements of chaos. Again in the rune poems we see mention of *Thor's* propensity to cause 'agony' in women.

There is ample evidence to support the thesis that giants are references to gods and also primal, titan-like spirits, or proto-deities. Here, in the OIRP, the image of *Thor* might be hinted at in this oblique kenning. The god of thunder and lightning would be well placed as a crag-dweller. *Thor* is also the enemy of giants and it has been pointed out that many of those he killed were in fact giantesses.

In myth *Thor's* mortal enemy is the *Midgard* serpent that circles the world under the ocean. At *Ragnorak* he will slay it, though it takes his life. This dragon in myth represents the elements of chaos and disorder over which the sky-god must win (a theme echoed in many other cultures). It is possible that his ultimate importance is reflected in the use of the name *Asa-Thor*. No other god is addressed thus, and it appears to enforce his original role as a supreme Deity amongst the *Aesir*.

The Hammer and ring are his sacred emblems. Miniature *Mjolnirs* have been found across ancient Scandinavia. The hammer was forged by dwarves at the behest of *Loki* and is the 'defender of the gods'. The ring may symbolically represent *Thor's* magical girdle, and such rings were used by his priests to swear oaths by. To strengthen the link between Thor and this rune comes another version of the OIRP:

Kvenna kvol, Kletta ibūi, Hamra heimramur.

Thurs is women's illness, cliff dweller, Hammering home amongst rocks.

References:

The Old English Rune Poem - A critical Edition - Maureen Halsall

Norse Mythology, a Guide to the Gods, Heroes, Rituals & Beliefs - John Lindow

Scandinavian Mythology - H.R Ellis

The Icelandic Rune Poem - R.I. Page

Runic & Hero Poems of the Old Teutonic Peoples -

DAVE MIGMAN

edited by Bruce Dickins

European Paganism - Ken Dowden

Ansuz/Áss

OERP

*(ōs) byþ ordfruma ælcre spærce,
wīsdōmes wraþu and witena frōfur
and eorla gehwām ēadnys and tōhiht.*

God (Odin) is the origin of all language
wisdom's foundation and the wise man's comfort
and to every hero a blessing and hope

OIRP

O er aldingautr, ok Ásgarðs Jofurr, ok Valhallar vísi.

O is ancient Gautr and Asgardr's warrior-king and

Vallhalla's ruler.

ONRP

Óss er flæstra færða, fær, en skalpr er sværða.

Estuary is the way for most onward journeys:
and the scabbard is the sword's.

As the OERP was written by a Christian scribe, a direct reference to Odin would seem like a huge clerical oversight (given the pains taken to eradicate Thor from the interpretation of the previous rune). Hence, some choose to interpret the OERP's first line as 'Mouth is the origin of all language'. I have chosen to use God, with reference to Odin/Woden here, for even if he is not directly mentioned in the OERP, his image remains in the reference to wisdom and heroes. The OIRP is more explicit in naming him, Ancient Gautr, another name for Odin. The ONRP reverts to the use of 'estuary'.

Not only did *Odin* discover the runes but he is the God of eloquence, the lord of poetry, wisdom and the source of all utterance. His hall, *Valhalla*, was the end-goal of his warriors. For there, they would drink and fight and feast and be reborn fresh and youthful every day. Such mythology hints at *Odin's* underworld connections, for he is also a god of death and storms, who parallels *Mercury* in many attributes. He has many names. As *Sigtyr*, he is 'god of victory', as *Val-fodhr*, he is 'father of the slain.' In many sagas, such as that of the *Volsungs*, it is *Odin* in person who comes to claim the lives of heroes. In the midst of *Sigmundr's* final battle, a one-eyed man appears and sticks the hero with a javelin. Thus *Odin* selects his army in preparation for *Ragnorak*. In many ways *Odin* possesses levels of insight and cunning that would make *Loki* shiver.

Etymologically, the root of *Odin's* name (*ódr*) means furor and rage. The root is related to frenzied poetic/prophetic inspiration. He was a sorcerer, possessing various magical items, and should his great spear pass above the heads of your army, then it was surely doomed. For it was also *Odin* who caused men to freeze in battle, netted as they were in his invisible fetters.

Odin is also a god who lusts after knowledge. He is a seeker, who not only travels *Midgard*, but through all the realms. Not only does he gain knowledge from *Mimir's* severed head, but pledges his eye for a sup at the well of knowledge. He also boasts, "If I see a strangled corpse swinging upon a tree, I cut and paint 'runes' on the corpse in such a way, that the man comes and talks with me." *Hávamál* (155). Indeed he is the god of the gallows, gaining insight from those who move beyond our world. *Huginn* and *Muninn*, his pet ravens, fly through the lands, bringing him information. From his throne, *Häsaeti*, he watches the worlds.

Evidently *Odin* possesses many shamanic qualities: the ritual hanging, shapeshifting, his spirit guides, his gazing into the worlds. Even the notion of *Odin* hanging on the world tree is deeply significant.

Knowledge, poetry and warfare are all vital to this Deity. In the earlier epoch of Germanic myth, he was *Wöðanaz/Woden*. The degenerated version, *Wode*, the leader of a mounted wild hunt, followed by thousands of spectres, echoes folk memories of the *Einherjar*.

As for the ONRP, *óss* is a homonym meaning river mouth and due to a change in the rune's phonetic value was altered from *Ansuz*.

I would place this rune as a 'speech rune', as mentioned in *Sigrdrífumál*.

Speech-runes learn, that none may seek
To answer harm with hate;
Well he winds and weaves them all, And sets them side by side,
At the judgment-place, when justice there
The folk shall fairly win.

Here the rune is invoked to be used at the *Thing*, which was a communal court or council where grievances were aired and judgement given.

Though this rune must have been seen as a good omen, perhaps, it was taken with an element of caution. *Odin* could be deceitful and sly. His was the constant sense of martial chaos, his delight appears to ensure that the princes kept fighting. He is the wise-man's counsel, and therefore, the canny person can avoid this darker, shadow aspect.

References:

The Old English Rune Poem - A critical Edition - Maureen Halsall

Rudiments of Runelore - Stephen Pollington

The Icelandic Rune Poem - R.I. Page

The Cult of Odin - Nora M. Chadwick

Runic & Hero Poems of the Old Teutonic Peoples - edited by Bruce Dickins

Raido/Reith

OERP

*(rād) byþ on recyde
rinca gehwylcum sēfte, and swīþhwæt
ðām ðe sitteþ onufan mēare mægenheardum
ofer mīlpaþas.*

Riding is for every man in the hall
easy and strenuous for he that sits upon
a powerful horse along the long roads

OIRP

DAVE MIGMAN

R er sitjandi sæla ok snúðig ferð ok jórs erfiði.

R is bliss of the seated and swift journey and horse's toil.

ONRP

Ræið Kveða rossom væstra, Reginn sló sværðet bæzta.

Riding they say is for horses worst,
Reginn hammered out the best sword.

In the OERP, the immediate impression is one of contrast. Riding is easy for men in the feast hall. This is contrasted with an arduous trek on a powerful steed. This works on different levels and has been interpreted in numerous ways. On one level, it could refer to the luxury of the material world, contrasted by the hardships of the undertaking of a spiritual journey or pilgrimage.

However the OIRP is more practical and terse, implying little more than the bliss of riding, the speed of the trip, countered by the burden of the beast. Here it appears to note that even though we might live in comfort, perhaps something else suffers for our ease. Some believe this rune, and the poems that allude to it, confer a mythological journey to the underworld and a journey between life and death. Therefore the rune itself might have also acted as a travel charm, offering protection in this life and the next.

The ONRP offers a cryptic clue, referencing *Reginn*, brother of *Ottr* and *Fafnir* from the *Volsung* saga. He is a dwarf, 'the mighty one' and he was known for his magical smithing abilities. It is treacherous *Reginn* who forged *Gram*, *Sigurdr's* sword, with which the hero smites the dragon, *Fafnir*. However *Reginn* still had designs on the hoard of treasure his brother guarded. The dying *dragon* warned *Sigurdr* not to take the gold as it would be his downfall, but *Sigurdr* took it anyway. *Reginn* made a soup with the cooked heart of the dragon, but *Sigurdr* accidentally tasted some. Suddenly he understood the chatter of the birds, who warned him of the dwarf's treacherous intentions. *Sigurdr* struck off *Reginn's* head with *Gram*. The reason the dwarf is mentioned in the ONRP may be because the perfect sword is forged by a flawed character; the line thus counterbalances the previous - the allusion that though riding is easy, for the rider, the horse suffers - there is always a price to be paid.

Raido is significantly different from the other Horse rune, *Ehwaz*. With *Raido*, the horse is symbiotic within a personal, individual journey. This could be metaphorical or literal. Here the horse represents the opportunities offered by such transport and the freedom thus afforded. In a time when transport options were much more limited, a horse meant more ground could be covered faster. However, everything has a price and we must be aware of the strain placed upon the mount.

The horse is also the metaphorical vehicle in a spiritual journey. In the *Hávamál*, *Odin* hangs on the world tree, named *Yggdrasil* - *Yggr's* mount. The ordeal is the medium by which *Odin* opens the portal through which *Mimir* (the font of all wisdom and memory) reveals the runes. Symbolically, horses were associated with the underworld and even *Sleipnir*, *Odin's* eight-legged steed, could cross the boundaries between life & death. In the tale *Baldr's* death, one of *Odin's* sons, *Hermod*, travels to the world of the dead on the magical steed.

Reference:

Teutonic Mythology Vol II - Viktor Rydberg

Runic & Hero Poems of the Old Teutonic Peoples - edited by Bruce Dickins

The Old English Rune Poem - Maureen Halsall

Kenaz/Kaun

OERP

(cēn) byþ cwicera gehwām cūþ on fyre,
blāc and beorhtlīc; byrneþ oftust
ðær hī æþelingas inne restaþ.

Torch is known to each living thing by fire
radiant and bright
it usually burns where nobles sit at ease

OIRP

K er barna bol ok bardagi ok holdfúa hús.

STONE MAD RUNES

Sore (Blain) is children's illness
and a battle journey
and putrescence's house

ONRP

Kaun er barna bolvan;
Bolgorver nán folvan.

Sore is the disfiguring of children;
adversity renders a person pale.

With regards to the OERP, some think that the reference alludes to the living and the dead. Taken literally, the stanza evokes a scene of ease, princes residing comfortably in the mead hall, lit with torches and warmed by fire. In death, the scene portrays nobles at rest on the funeral pyre, the flaming torch is that which will send them to Valhalla. Such accounts of funerary boats and pyres are well attested in literary and archaeological sources. As most runes have meaning on various levels they often reveal a shadow side. I suggest that it might refer to both living and dead states. In Valhalla the warrior elite feast, in a bright hall lit by many torches. Valhalla mirrors the idealistic warrior life beyond the grave.

Fire was also seen as purifying and sacred in many religions. Fire possesses a dual transformative nature. Fire destroys and yet is vital for life, especially in a cold climate. Fire, when domesticated, provides light and heat, it is radiant and nurturing. Its power can be harnessed in forge or by fuel. Yet the element is its own master, it is insatiable unless boundaried, is greedy and if uncared for will destroy and decimate. We must remember that the act of destruction is part of a process, a process that is as natural as death. Old forest must burn to yield the way for new life.

The act of cremating a body on a funeral pyre was a sacred act of transformation: taking the corporeal body and turning it into smoke and ash had a metaphoric symbolism that was observable physically and believed spiritually.

A variant to this rune does appear in another rune list as Keen or Brave, which might tie into the ONRP & OIRP reference to Blain or sore. The reference here might be that an ailment must be carefully monitored, and tended, as with a fire, or it may become a bigger problem. The sore may become putrescent. This would have been particularly pertinent to a time before penicillin was discovered.

Illumination also figures with this rune in the sense of creativity. The creative fires are a metaphorical reference to the destructive and creative forces which exist within mankind.

Reference:

Runic & Hero Poems of the Old Teutonic Peoples - Edited by Bruce Dickins

The Old English Rune Poem - Maureen Halsall

The Icelandic Rune Poem - R.I. Page

Gebo/Gyfu

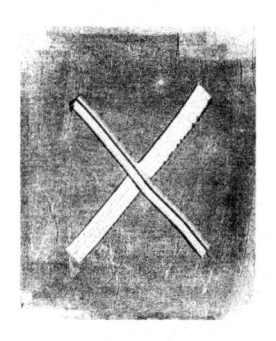

OERP

*(gyfu) gumena byþ gleng and herenys
wraþu and wyrþscype; and wræcna gehwām
ār and ætwist, ðe byþ ōþra lēas.*

*Gift is an honour and a grace of men
a support and adornment*
and for all the dispossessed
it is a help and a means of survival, when they have no other.

This symbol is absent from the ONRP & OIRP. It could be that in the pared down Younger Futhark, the similarity between Feoh and Gebo was too close, whereas the AS adopted it to fit their world view. The root of this rune is *ge - 'gift'. As mentioned in Feoh, gift-giving was a tradition that ennobled and honoured giver and receiver. Gifting strengthened communal ties and instigated mutual respect. As the old adage goes, a gift demands a gift.

It is quite possible that the essence of 'gift' here was Christianised in favour of charity, referring to communal support and reliance on others. However, *Odin* was sometimes portrayed as a beggar, even though he ruled the lands and his wealth was immeasurable. In this guise, he would test the generosity of his people, and the value of this virtue would be rewarded. In this aspect he is a godfather of the poor, bestowing gifts where needed.

There are gifts that are immaterial too. Gifts of love and affection are obvious, but we also say that people are born for example, blessed with the gift of the gab, or the gift of beauty. In the past such gifts were perceived as blessings from the gods, or fates. *Freyr* may bless some with the gift of beauty, *Bragi* others with the gift of the gab. Gifts were given to the old gods in form of libation and sacrifice and gifts were bestowed upon the people in return. In this way gifts connected the world of the mundane with that of the sacred, reinforcing the reciprocal nature of this relationship.

Reference:

The Gift - Lewis Hyde

The Old English Rune Poem - Maureen Halsall

Runic & Hero Poems of the Old Teutonic Peoples - Bruce Dickins

Wunjo/Wyn

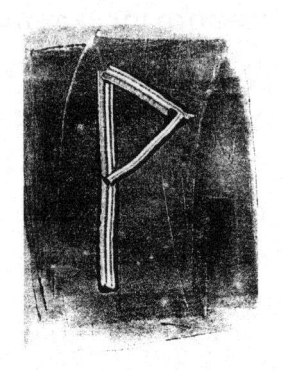

OERP

(wyn) ne brūceþ ðe can wēana lyt,
sāres and sorge,
and him sylfa hæfþ bæld and blysse
and ēac byrga geniht.

Happiness he cannot enjoy who knows little woe,
pain and sorrow,
and has for himself
wealth and joy
and sufficient protection too.

In Wunjo, we have joy but this is offset, in that to know joy you must also know sorrow. Nobody can exist in a state of pure joy for their entire life. Such a life would not have value, as the value can only be appreciated through knowing sorrow.

This concept is adequately displayed in the story of the death of *Baldr*. *Odin's* son is great and wise, beautiful to behold and brings the gods great joy. Perfection must be finite, balance must be maintained. Through deceit, *Loki* has *Baldr* killed by his brother, *Höd*. Overcome by grief, *Baldr's* wife throws herself upon his pyre. Meanwhile *Hermod*, another of *Odin's* progeny, rides *Sleipnir* to *Hel* to retrieve the stricken god. *Hel* makes a deal with *Hermod* that if he can prove that there are none that would not weep for *Baldr*, then she will release him. All would weep for *Baldr*, save a single old woman, who refuses. Thus *Baldr* remains in *Hel*. Many suspect the old woman was *Loki* in disguise. *Baldr* is too perfect, and nature seeks balance, the joy he represents is cruelly ripped away from those who loved him. This concept is encompassed by the OERP.

This rune stands, not only for self-contentment, but also the happiness of security, a joy of being protected by clan and community. This is happiness found in tribal, communal wealth. It is secured, safe inside the enclosure, with strong warriors nearby, with deities placated with libation and chieftains who prefer peace over war. This could only be a good rune in any lot and obviously a significantly sought after symbol. The rune was used by clerical, Christian scribes in AS texts to mean simply rejoice and joy.

Sequentially, *Wyn* brings us to the 'happy ending' of the first *ætt*. What began with a reference to communal wealth ends in the sanctuary of the tribal group. *Freyr's ætt* is suitably framed by community and each rune is grounded in aspects of every-day life. Yet each possesses a spiritual aspect too. *Freyr* is very much the god of the homestead and farming communities and this is reflected in this *ætt* - physically and spiritually. It is interesting to note that the upbeat refrain of this rune is paralleled in the other *ætts*, with *Sól* and *Dagaz/Othalo*. In fact *Freyr's ætt* is almost cyclical, a journey from *Feoh* to *Wyn*, ending with the emphasis on strength in the community and the pleasures afforded therein.

Reference:

The Old English Rune Poem - Maureen Halsall

Norse Mythology: A Guide to the Gods, Heroes, Rituals & Beliefs - John Lindow

Runic & Hero Poems of the Old Teutonic Peoples - Edited by Bruce Dickins

Hagal's ætt

Hagalz/Hagal

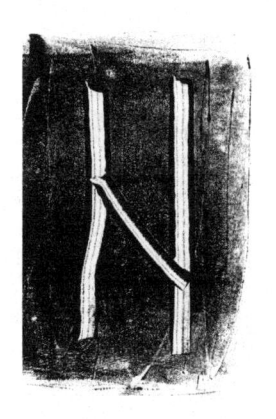

OERP

(hægl) byþ hwītust corna;
hwyrft hit of heofones lyfte,
wealcaþ hit windes scūra;
weorþeþ hit tō wætere syððan.

Hail is whitest of corn
from heaven's height it whirls
wind blown
it becomes water after

DAVE MIGMAN

OIRP

h er kaldakorn ok knappa drifa ok snaka sott.

Hail is cold seed
and a sleet shower
and snake's illness

ONRP

Hagall er kaldastr korna;
Kristr skóp hæimenn forna

Hail is the coldest of seeds;
Christ shaped the heavens in fore times

Archaeologically, Hagal has been found inscribed on spears and pendants. It might have been to invoke the power of the hail storm as a hail of spears. In the ONRP, the reference to Christ is obviously due to the creed of the scribe. Perhaps originally, there was some other meaning to be countered with a stress on the Almighty Yahweh's hand in creation? The coldest seed hints at an agricultural kenning, perhaps an inference to Hail's destructive power within an agricultural society. It might also reference the idea that the seed or grain is the beginning of something, in this case the start of a blizzard. The inference is that shelter must be sought.

Hagal begins the new family of runes after *Freyr's ætt*. Although some attest to this being *Hagal's ætt* and therefore referencing a deity, there is no historical reference to *Hagal* as a god. The OIRP mentions that Hail is a serpent's sickness. This might be an allusion to the god *Thor* and his mortal enemy the world serpent, through whose bite *Thor* dies, but not before he slays it. As I mentioned in my chapter on the *ættir*, it may be that this central family was altered. Perhaps, at one time, this *ætt* belonged to the god credited with bringing the runes into the world - *Odin*. The ONRP makes specific reference to the heavens being the creation of Christ. Again this could be a stress on the part of the cleric to enforce Christian creed over something more recognisably pagan. It has always puzzled me that, given *Odin's* obvious connection to runelore that he wasn't referenced more. Another clue lies in the fourth rune of *Freyr's ætt*, *Ass/Ansuz* - which in the OIRP is implicit in naming *Odin*, as *Old Gautr*. The scribe who wrote the ONRP, however, makes no such allusions.

An awe-like recognition of transformation features in the OERP. The negativity of hail is turned into a positive and delights in the transformation of icy seeds into water. A transition of states is at play here, not only from solid to liquid, but also from sky to earth. The rune is raw and elemental, setting a precedent of the storm to come, and the tranquility that often follows the storm. The transience of adversity is evident in this rune: if you can weather the storm it will pass overhead.

References:

The Old English Rune Poem - Maureen Halsall

The Norwegian Rune Poem in context: Style, Structure and Imagery - Veronka Szöke

Runic Amulets and Magic Objects - Mindy Macleod and Bernard Mees

The Icelandic Rune Poem - R.I. Page

Runic and hero Poems of the Old Teutonic Peoples - edited by Bruce Dickins

Isa/Iss

OERP

(īs) byþ oferceald, ungemetum slidor;
glisnaþ glæshlūttur gimmum gelīcust;
flōr forste geworuht, fæger ansyne.

Ice is too cold and extremely slippery
glass clear it glistens most like gems
a floor made of frost
fair in appearance

OIRP

I er árborkr ok unnar þekja

ok feigra manna fär.

I is river-bark and wave's thatch
and doomed men's downfall.

ONRP

Ís kollum brú bræiða;
Blindan þarf at læiða.

Ice is called a bridge road;
the blind need to be led.

In the frozen winters of the northern world, Ice is a thing of both beauty and hardship. The allusion in the ONRP and OIRP to the span of a frozen river being like a bridge hints at the power of ice. As with all the runes, it hints at a deeper layer of meaning. In Nordic creation myth, Ice is the primal creative element. From the rivers known as Élivágar, which turned into a lava like flow of icy fermentation, ice and frost filled the void, Ginnungagap. Ymir, the giant from whose body the bones of the world were fashioned, was also know as the father of frost giants, and it is from this icy spew that he emerged. Ice then may seem to imbue the world with sterility, but to the ancient Scandinavian world, this ice was the very stuff of life.

Ice also possesses a purity and the form of the rune, a simple line, is very stark and precise. It has also been suggested that the rune functions as a pictogram, alluding to the blindman in the ONRP, who needs a staff. As a gruesome side, it is worth noting that blinding was a form of punishment during the Germanic migrations.

In both instances, cosmological or mundane, the rune calls for wariness, and yet offers a visual aesthetic that pleases the soul. Ice is liquid become solid, and it can symbolise lack of flow. In the positive sense this can be stillness or resting, or it can hint at stasis and being on hold.

References:

The Icelandic Rune Poem - R.I. Page

The Norwegian Rune Poem in Context: Style, Structure and Imagery - Veronka Szöke -

The Old English Rune Poem - Maureen Halsall

Runic & Hero Poems of the Old Teutonic Peoples - Edited by Bruce Dickins

Nauthiz/Nauth

OERP

(nyd) byþ nearu on brēostan;
weorþeþ hī ðēah oft niþa bearnum
tō helpe and tō hæle gehwæþre,
gif hī his hlystaþ æror.

Need is hard by the heart
yet for men's sons it often becomes
a help and healing if they need it before.

OIRP

N er byjar bra ok bungr kostr ok vassamlig verk.

N is a bondswoman's grief and rough conditions and soggy toil.

ONRP

Nauðr gerer næppa koste;
Noktan kælr í froste

Need renders little choice;
the naked will freeze in the frost

On the horn thou shalt write, and the backs of thy hands,
And Need shalt mark on thy nails.
Thou shalt bless the draught, and danger escape,

(*Sigrdrífumál*, verse 7 . Trans. Bellows).

In all the rune poems, this rune appears to infer the quality of suffering, drudgery and toil. However, only the OERP offers hope. Here, need is seen as a stepping stone to healing. Sometimes we must fall before we rise again. This could be seen as a spiritual or physical trial, a test to steel the will. The OIRP appeals to our sense of empathy, for the naked will freeze in the frost, and therefore our hospitality is invoked.

This rune appears in many Germanic and Scandinavian inscriptions, sometimes alongside others in formulae. In a runic love charm, nine N runes are listed. *Risti eg þér / ása átta / nauðir níu / þussa þrettán.. This translates as : I carve you eight ás-runes, nine nauthiz-runes, thirteen þurs.* From another amulet comes: *Ek þurs seg þriu, naudr niu (I say three giants, nine needs).* Even the hilariously titled Fart Charm from the 16th Century grimoire, entitled *The Galdrabók,* calls for: *eight ás runes, nine*

Nuathiz and thirteen Thorn/Thurs runes. Other healing charms appear to invoke the lord of giants (*Thor* and the Thurs/Thorn rune) while cussing the wolf (a metaphor for illness) with nine needs (*Nauthiz*).

The origin of the word could well be linked to the dead, corpses and even ghouls. English need comes from the OE *nē-, nēo-* dead. Gothic *Naus* and OI *nár* both refer to a corpse. Could this be the rune which *Odin* inscribes to reanimate dangling corpses? Was this rune part of the *valgaldr*, or death raising charms? Necromancy was part and parcel of myth and magic in Northern Europe even beyond the Medieval period. In Saxo's *Grammaticas Gesta Danorum* the tale is told of the giantess, *Harthgrepa*, who carves certain spells on pieces of wood and places them beneath a corpses stiff tongue. The corpse is revived and foretells the future. *Nauthiz* may have formed a vital part of a trinity in magical formulae: Gods, giants or *Thor* and ancestral spirits.

References:

The n-Rune & Nordic Charm Magic - Stephen A. Mitchell

The Old English Rune Poem - Maureen Halsall

Runic and Hero Poems of the Old Teutonic Peoples - Edited by Bruce Dickins

The Norwegian Rune Poem In Context: Style, Structure and Imagery - Veronka Szöke

The Icelandic Rune Poem - R.I. Page

Contexts of the Oldest Runic Inscriptions - Tineke Looijenga

Runic Amulets & Magic Objects - Mindy Macleod and Bernard Mees

Jera/Ar

OERP

*(ġēr) byþ gumena hiht, ðon God læteþ,
hālig heofones cyning,
hrūsan syllan beorhte blēda
beornum and ðearfum.*

Harvest is Men's hope when god allows
- holy king of heaven
the earth to give up
fair fruits to warriors and to wretches

OIRP

DAVE MIGMAN

A er gumna gæði ok gott sumar.

Year/harvest is men's bounty
and a good summer
and a full grown field

ONRP

Ár er gumna góðe;
Get ek at orr var Fróðe.

Year/harvest is men's bounty;
I guess that generous was Frodhi.

After winter comes summer and the wonderful yields of harvest. In OE, this was known as Hærvestmonaþ and was celebrated in the month of September. The rune refers to a fruitful and bounteous harvest. A 7th Century runestone from Sweden makes use of the rune in the following manner: niu habrumR, niu hangistumR, HaþuwulfR gaf J (nine goats, nine stallions, HaþuwulfR gave Year). Obviously a statement of how Hathuwulfr made ample provision for a bounteous harvest. A good harvest is reliant on good preparation. If you put the work in, you reap the reward. However, agriculture is at the mercy of the elements and as such fate has a part to play in whether a bountiful harvest is delivered. This works on a metaphorical as well as a literal level.

In the ONRP, a mythical character is referenced. According to Snorri Sturluson, *Frodhi* was a ruler during the reign of the Roman Emperor, Augustus. It was said under his reign the roads and highways were devoid of bandits and outlaws. It was a time of plenty, when hunger was unknown. Only the ONRP mentions him though, and this may be due to the Christian pretensions of the author. Christ was born during Augustus' time. The allusion to Christ is more apparent in the OERP, in which his name is invoked. However, these appear to gloss over the original heathen deity concealed behind the symbolism. This implies *Freyr* who was known as *Inn-Frodi*, meaning 'the Prolific One' and *Árgud* - the god of the harvest. (For more on *Freyr* see *Ingwaz*).

Sequentially *Harvest* here is strategically placed, it follows the dormant winter period of scarcity, storms and need. The endurance of the lean months is a necessary part of the cycle of the year. Nature worship in the Northern European tradition is evident in the placing of festivities within the calendar. In countries such as Scandinavia and Britain, where the climates of summer and winter are opposites, there is necessarily a deeper respect of the elements. In agricultural societies the importance of preparation cannot be stressed enough. These could be times of feast or famine. The Anglo-Saxon calendar reveals how the year was systematically arranged to celebrate the old deities, whilst ensuring crops were sown, harvested on time and cattle slaughtered for the winter months.

References;

The Icelandic Rune Poem - R.I. Page

The Norwegian Rune Poem in Context: Style, Structure & Imagery - Veronka Szöke -

The Old English Rune Poem - Maureen Halsall

Runic and Hero Poems of the Old Teutonic Peoples - Edited by Bruce Dickins

Contexts of the Oldest Runic Inscriptions - Tineke Looijenga

Scandinavian Mythology - H.R Ellis

The Viking Way - Neil S. Price

European Paganism - Ken Dowden

Eihwaz/Yr

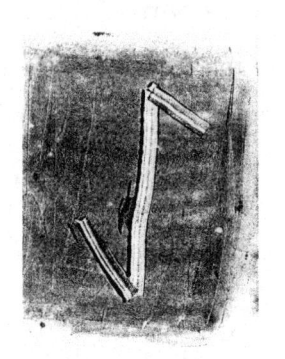

OERP

(ēoh) byþ ūtan unsmēþe trēow,
heard hrūsan fæst, hyrde fryes,
wyrtrumun underwreþyd,
wynan on ēþle.

Yew is rough tree outside
hard, earthfast, fire's keeper
underpinned with roots
a joy in the homeland

OIRP

tvijbendtur bogi, bardaga gagn, fyfu farbauti

Yew is a bent bow
a fragile iron
the arrow's Farbauti

ONRP

Yr er vetrgronstr viða;
Vænt er brenne, at sviða.

Yew is the winter-greenest wood;
and is found wanting, when it burns, to ignite.

Yews have a legacy in both Celtic and Norse mythology. Some contend that Yggdrasil was a yew, not an ash. Yggdrasil was the greenest tree and failed to burn despite the terrors of Ragnorak. In the World Tree's branches the nine worlds clustered and its roots led down to Hel and the wells of prophecy, fate and intellect. That a sacred Yew grew at Upsalla, and is mentioned by Adam of Bremen, strengthens this claim. The otherworldly and associations with death are widely noted in relation to yews. The great age of yews may also have been a reason for the tree's association with death. Some trees have been known to reach ages of over 2000 years. It is a common tree to see in Christian graveyards and this tradition comes from Pre-Christian times. This is reflected in the OERP, where roots can be taken to suggest links with the underworld and ancestry. There is a solidity referenced in the description in this poem, a recognition of its endurance.

Scholars are still at odds as to the actual

phonetic value of this rune, and it only makes an appearance in runic inscriptions after the 4th Century AD. However, we have evidence of Celtic and Germanic tribes called the *Eburones* (People of the yew), *Eburovices, Eburobriga, Eburmagus* and *Eburodunum*. Yew wands have been discovered that were marked with runes from *Frisia*, pointing to the wood's use in magic and ritual. Longbows were also made from this durable wood and several have been found in Archaeological sites across Germanic realms and Scandinavia.

Faubauti was *Loki's* father, a giant whose name means anger-striker, potentially referring to the power of the yew bow. *Loki,* then, would be the arrow, hinting at the somewhat deceitful nature of the use of bows in battle. Their use was less up close and personal. Archery may well have been frowned on by those in cults of *Woden/Odin*, in which close combat was the essence of bravery and martial prowess. The OIRP poem plays with contrasts here. The bow is called a fragile iron yet compared with the giant's strength. The overall impression is one of deceptive appearances. The arrow is fine and bears a keen point, but it is of little consequence without the power of the bow. And still, the bow also needs someone to draw it and take aim. Each component is reduced in power without the sum of its parts. Yet each part is vital in its place, weak without the others, strong in union.

References;

Contexts Of The Oldest Runic Inscriptions - Tineke Looijenga

Ullr - A God On The Edge Of Memory - John Julian Molin

The Ancient Yew; A History of Taxus Baccata - Robert Beven Jones

The Icelandic Rune Poem - R.I. Page

The Old English Rune Poem - Maureen Halsall

Runic & Hero Poems of the Old Teutonic Peoples - Edited by Bruce Dickin

Peorð

OERP

*(peorð) byþ symble plega and hlehter
wlancum....., ðār wigan sittaþ on bēorsele
blīþe ætsomne.*

Gaming is always play and laughter
to proud men... where warriors sit
in the beerhall happily together.

There seems to be so little written about this rune in the sources. Its exact meaning remains disputed. It is often interpreted as gaming or dicing - some translations have it as chess-man. It is clear that the OERP invokes a cheery scene, perhaps contrasting the reality of proud warriors with the frivolity of their play. This may indicate the social nature of a dice game, rather than the seriousness of chess. Dice games have been played since very ancient times. Bone dice have been found across ancient Europe. The idea of chance and fate are two opposed concepts. One premises that the roller has the ability to tap into the universal chaos and receive random results. The other suggests a predetermined outcome, strongly bound by ideas of

Fate or wyrd. That is that destiny is already fixed. However a third principle is relevant to both these ideas, or viewpoints. That is the belief in luck. People across the globe have worn amulets, charms, sprigs of certain plants, etc, in the hope of enhancing this mysterious quality, while some are just 'born lucky'. Luck or fortune come into its element in these types of gameplay. As a pictogram it bears the appearance of an empty dicing cup.

Chess was a development of the *Tafl*, or table games, such as the Norse *Hnefatafl* and *Halatafl*. These require a different technique, involving strategising. Players must contemplate their moves, planning turns in advance. Although the element of chance still exists the games are very honed to the experience and character of the players. Chess, and similar games, feature in myths in a symbolic sense. Indeed the idea of commanding an army, represented by games pieces across a symbolic battlefield, raises notions of the microcosm reflecting the macrocosm. The metaphor is very rich and players assume a godlike status while they play.

The ambiguity as to the exact nature and meaning of this rune lends itself neatly to the notions of chance and fate. Either way it suggests that unseen forces are at play, and events are out of your hands.

References;

Runic & Hero Poems of the Old Teutonic Peoples - Edited by Bruce Dickins

The Old English Rune Poem - Maureen Halsall

Algiz

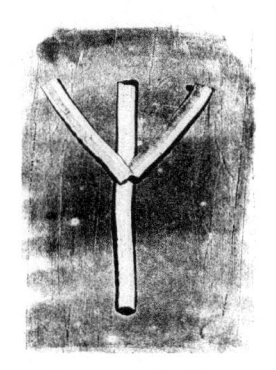

OERP

(eolhx) secg eard hæfþ oftust on fenne,
wexeð on wature; wundaþ grimme,
blōde brēneð beorna gehwylcne
ðe him ænigne onfeng gedēð.

Elk-grass most often dwells in a fen,
grows in water, harshly wounds,
marks with blood any warrior
who tries to take it.

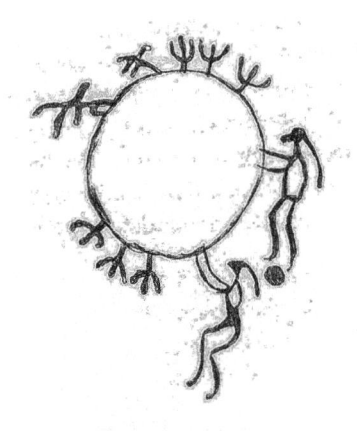

This rune is problematic for a number of reasons. Mainly this boils down to the translation of the name. OERP is the only rune poem which features it. Part of the problem is that the phonetic value of its origins; Z/R in Germanic was no longer in use in Britain by the time the poem was transcribed. It appears that the assigning of the "x" sound was arbitrary and based on Latin influence.

To further compound the phonetic issue, the meaning is also difficult to decipher. The modern usage, as protection, comes from speculation and certain interpretations that the original meaning was 'Elk' and therefore protection. This is heightened by the prolific 'Helm of Awe' (*ægishjálmur*) symbol. This sigil appears as a binding of *Algiz* in a cross form (in Spell 8 from the 16th Century book, The *Galdrabók*, to win a girl's love). In the Huld Manuscript, the rune appears as a composite in numerous sigils, including the *Brynslustafir* (Whet sign) and *Vegvisir*.

The *ægishjálmur* is also problematic. In Stephen Flowers' translation of Icelandic black art sigils (stemming from the late 16th - 18th Centuries AD) it does not appear in the form that is currently en vogue. This appears to stem from something else, more modern, but I cannot trace the source.

Many texts point to the name of this symbol being included in *Fáfnismál* (stanza 16). *Ægishjalm* means helmet of protection. *Hjalm* = Helmet, *ægis* comes from the Greek, and is synonymous with protection. It is interesting to note that the symbol was also probably associated with serpent/dragon myths. *Athena's Aegis* was a shield bearing the head of the gorgon. Obviously some protective quality is assumed by the *Fáfnismál* reference but it is the fact that it is worn by *Fáfnir*, the dragon, that perhaps has led to the conclusion that this is the same imagery.

Still, this does not prove that this symbol, now used frequently in association with Viking art, is the same. To my knowledge, it does not exist in early Germanic or later Viking art. I have researched symbols for over 20 years and I've never seen it thus in archaeological finds (Answers on a postcard please if you can provide evidence to the contrary). In my opinion, the inference is simply a helmet, possibly forged by *Reginn, Fáfnir's* treacherous brother. Flowers postulates that this symbol is some sort of a covering with the motif placed over the third eye. This is a beguiling idea but lacks supporting evidence.

The sound of this rune had altered by the Viking age, thus it is also *Yr*, yew or yew bow. In this form it is reversed - I am leaving it out, given that this is the meaning for *Eihwaz*. In the ONRP, this symbol is placed for *Maðr*, which is the *Man/Mannaz*. Again I leave this from here. These appear to be later, *Younger Futhark* developments and are not the focus of this work.

If the rune was originally *Elk*, this might explain the symbol as a pictogram of an antler. But every translation I delved into has it as *Elk-sedge*. The allusion in the OERP is that even if a warrior grabs it, it will harshly wound them. Again the idea does suggest a protective quality. I envisage something that might be deemed fragile actually turning out much tougher than it is, the deception of appearances, endurance and tenaciousness. Something that will not yield, no matter how inconsequential it appears at first glance.

References:

The Galdrabók, An Icelandic Grimoire - Stephen Flowers

The Old English Rune Poem - Frederick George Jones Jnr.

The Old English Rune Poem - Maureen Halsall

Runic & Hero Poems of the Old Teutonic Peoples - Edited by Bruce Dickins

Sigel/Sol

OERP

*(sigel) sēmannum symble biþ on hihte,
ðonn hī hine feriaþ ofer fisces beþ,
oþ hī brimhengest bringeþ tō lande.*

Sun to seamen is always a hope
when they travel over the fish's bath
until the sea-steed brings them to land

OIRP

S er skyja skjoldr ok skinandi roðull.

S is clouds' shield and shining halo.

ONRP

Sól er landa ljóme;
Lúti ek helgum dóme.

The sun is the land's light;
I bow to holy judgement.

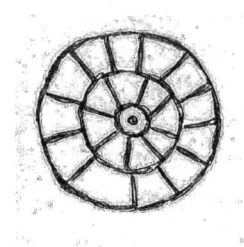

As we started this set with a hailstorm, so we end with the glory of the sun. The OIRP literally states this as a fact. The sun is the antithesis of ice, of which Hagal heralds. Of course the ONRP again reflects the ideals of the Christian scribe who wrote upon the vellum in the Middle-Ages. However, it has been noted that the final line reflects other heathen skalds to the sun.

Sol was the daughter of *Mundilfare* and she rode the horses that pulled the chariot of the sun. This type of imagery is common amongst the IE peoples, but it is only in the Scandinavian/Germanic traditions that the sun appears as a goddess rather than a masculine god. In ancient Germanic tradition the sun-wheel was an iconic image and many examples have been found. The famous Trundholm Sun Disc, now housed in the National Museum of Denmark, is a ritual artefact that shows the sun disc in all its glory, drawn by a beautiful horse, all set on wheels evocative of other solar symbols (sun cross). The sun was an emblem of great power and virtue. It brought fortune, light, luck and strength. However, *Sol* herself does not appear to be the sun. Like her brother, *Mani*, her task is to drive the horses that pull it through the sky. She and her brother are relentlessly pursued by two malevolent wolves.

Some question the relevance of the OERP reference to the ocean and sea-faring, others suggest its relevance came in providing protection to sea-farers. The root of this may be connected to ancient bronze-age carvings. In many petroglyphs from Scandinavia, ships are portrayed with sun symbols on their masts. Sometimes the ship is flanked by bird-like prows. The imagery most likely reflects a myth concerning the dynamics of the solar disc, and where it went each night. The sun being borne across the ocean on a boat is also reflected in ancient Egyptian mythology, where *Ra* journeys through the duat in his sun-barge each night. Even into the age of Christianity, the sun was viewed as divine and many viewed it as a manifestation of this divinity. Given that the sun is the source of all life on earth, it is not surprising that it is recognised in this way cross culturally. *Sowilo* as the rune of the sun is indisputably powerful in a positive way.

Sun to seamen is always a hope through orienting, east as it rises and west as it falls. It represents the optimism of the sun emerging following the earlier struggles of this *ætt*.

References;

The Norwegian Rune Poem in Context: Style, Structure and Imagery - Veronka Szöke

The Old English Rune Poem - Maureen Halsall

Teutonic Mythology Vol III - Viktor Rydberg

A reader In Comparative Indo-European Religion - Ranko Matasović

Runic & Hero Poems of the Old Teutonic Peoples - Bruce Dickins

Tyr's ætt

Tiwaz/Tyr

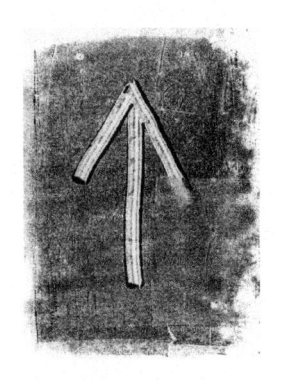

OERP

(Tīr) biþ tācna sum;
healdeð trywa wel wiþ æþelingas;
ā biþ on færylde ofer nihta genipu;
næfre swīceþ.

Tyr is one of the signs, holds faith well with noblemen, on a journey is always above night's gloom, never fails

OIRP

t er einhendr ass ok ulfs leifar.

t is one-handed god and wolf's left-overs.

ONRP

Tyr er œinendr ása; opt værða smiðr blása

Tyr is the one-handed god;
oft will a smith be blowing

Winning-runes learn, if thou longest to win,
And the runes on thy sword-hilt write;
Some on the furrow, and some on the flat,
And twice shalt thou call on Tyr.

(Sigrdrìfumàl verse 6, Bellows Trans.)

It was Tyr who placed his hand in Fenrir's mouth, effectively sacrificing his hand in order to bind the beast. His sense of integrity, strength and fortitude are expressed in the OERP. These lines also hint at some obscure astrological significance (possibly Mars, his Roman counterpart). His sign, or star, was obviously invoked for the purposes of navigation. The literal translation of Tīr is guiding star although Tyr also meant 'god'. Tir, or Tiwaz, is an ancient god, who most likely predates Odin. However as the latter's popularity rose, Tyr was relegated to the status of a minor god*. His day is Tuesday in our calendar, OE Tiwesdœg, which interestingly corresponds to the Italian Martedi, Day of Mars.

Tyr was once known for his wisdom, for wise men were called *Tyr-wise*, just as readily as brave men were known to be as valiant as *Tyr*. He is a god of law and justice. His parentage is attributed to the all-wise *Hymir* and a giantess. It has been suggested that taking the cosmological order of this rune, it references *Fehu/Feoh*. The inference here being an antithesis to the harmony invoked by *Feoh*. With *Tyr*, *Fenrir* lurks in his shadow, lips flecked with the war god's blood. Hence here reference is made to *Ragnorak*, in which 'brother battles brother and sister turns upon sister'. A terrible reverse of the community invoked by *Feoh*.

The phrase 'Wolf's left-overs' degrades *Tyr* and devalues his god-like status. This reflects the rise of the cult of *Woden* in the Viking era, eclipsing the previous importance of Tyr to the Germanic tribes. Here too, a precedent is set for the twilight of the gods: they are fallible, they can fall, they die. *Odin*, *Thor* and *Tyr* all perish at *Ragnorak* (*Tyr* faces *Garm***).

The allusion to the Smith blowing in the ONRP is uncertain, but could well reference the magical art of a smith making a replacement hand for the deity. This notion of the lost hand (and replacement), appears in Celtic mythology in the guise of *Nuada*, an Irish-Celtic god of war. Associations have been drawn between the two. He lost his hand in battle and it was replaced with one fashioned in silver. The loss of a hand is relevant here, as both were degraded by this disfigurement. *Odin* sacrifices an eye for knowledge, *Tyr* his hand for honour and justice.

Tyr was the victory rune, carved upon swords and weapons. It appears that invocation of his name was part of this process. The arrow like pictogram of this rune is often likened to a spear, reinforcing *Tyr's* martial aspect and judicial combat. In addition, arrows are directional and this could corroborate the navigational significance of the rune. A further possibility is that the symbol could also represent *Irmisul*, the World tree used by Germanic tribes such as the Saxons. In this sense then the rune represents ideals of justice, law and victory.

References:

The Eldar Eddas of Snorre Sturlusson - Editied by I.A Blackwell

Corpus Poeticum Boreale Vol 1&2 - Gudbrand Vigfusson & F. York Powell

The Old English Rune Poem - Maureen Halsall

The Icelandic Rune Poem - R.I. Page

Runic & Hero Poems of the Old Teutonic Peoples - Edited by Bruce Dickins

Tyr is called *Baldr's* Brother by Snorri, making him a son of *Odin* in the Scandinavian tradition.

** *Garm* is a wolf who mirrors *Fenrir* and is also called 'the greatest monster'. Perhaps alluding to an earlier myth in which *Tyr* took a more prominent role before *Odin's* cult rose to the fore.

Beorc/Bjarkan

OERP

(beorc) byþ blēda lēas;
bereþ efne swā ðēah tānas būtan tūdder;
biþ on telgum wlitig, hēah on helme,
hrysted fægere; geloden lēafum, lyfte getenge.

Birch is fruitless, yet bears
shoots without seeds, is pretty in its branches,
high in its spread, fair adorned, laden with leaves
touching the sky

OIRP

blomgat tre, litel hnisla, j ast saemiligs uidar

blossoming tree, little sprig, of delightful wood.

ONRP

Bjarkan er laufgrostr líma; Loki bar flærða tíma.

Birch is leaf-greenest of limbs;
Loki bore treachery's fortune
(alt = Loki was fortunate in his deceit)

Under various guises and appellations, the birch is a goddess of fertility and growth. This goddess appears as Freyja in the Scandinavian myths. In the form of the birch, she was celebrated as the queen of May and decorated with flowers and ribbons. Maytime Festivals were held to honour the community and the ancestors and usher in the summer. These celebrations also involved fertility rites. May is a season of immeasurable beauty, a time of ritual and celebration.

Freyja was one of the *Vanir*, the ancient order of benevolent deities, associated with nature and the land. She was daughter of *Njord*, sister of *Freyr*. Like *Odin*, *Freyja* was known by many names. She appears to parallel *Frigg* in certain aspects (whom Snorri declares is her equal in nobility), and both were compared to the goddess *Venus*. *Freyja's* husband, *Odr*, has been compared to *Odin*. Even the constellation, Orion, was known as *Frigga*, but later became *Freyja's* spinning Wheel.

Freyja was instrumental in teaching the arts

of *siedr* to the *Aesir*, when she was offered as hostage during the termination of enmity between *Vanir* and *Aesir*. She could don a falcon cloak, shapeshifting into bird form and it is said her tears were droplets of red gold. She travelled in a chariot pulled by cats. She was also the head of the *Valkyries*, the powerful female warrior 'spirits'.

The original *Freyja** was a goddess of fertility, confused with similar archetypes across the spread of the Indo-European expansion, and emanating from earlier proto-deities. As time moved on, so *Freyja* acquired the trappings of Viking society, including their love for the poetic form - *Freyja* is said to have been a lover of erotic poetry. She was sometimes reviled by *Loki* for her supposed promiscuity, and in one tale she lays with four dwarves in exchange for a beautiful necklace. She was invoked by lovers and the lovelorn alike.

Loki's mention in the ONRP may reference the death of *Baldr*, engineered by his deceit. *Loki* is known as a trickster and was treated with caution by the other gods in all the legends, however, there is always an element of grudging respect for his cleverness in fooling others. The reference is not elaborated on and here appears out of sync with the other poems for this rune.

Beorc is *Freyja's* rune, and thus represents fertility, magic and the onset of summer, love and poetry. Sequentially it counters the masculinity of the previous rune, *Tyr*. The placing of this interesting pair feels wholly intentional. Balance is sought. This rune embodies the feminine side of nature, from the blossoming to the ripening and bearing of fruit. As referenced in the OERP, the birch is a fruitless tree but is beautiful in its reach and form.

References:

The folklore of Plants - T.F. Thiselton-Dyer

The Icelandic Rune Poem - R.I. Page

Runic & Hero Poems of the Old Teutonic Peoples - Edited by Bruce Dickins

The Norwegian Rune Poem in Context: Style, Structure and Imagery - Veronka Szöke

The Old English Rune Poem - Maureen Halsall

Irish Trees, Myths, Legends & Folklore - Niall Mac Coitir

Myth, Materiality & Lived Religion - (Edited) K.Wikstöm, P. Rova, A Nordberg, O. Sundquist, T. Zachrisson

Corpus Poeticum Boreale Vol 1&2 - Gudbrand Vigfusson & F. York Powell

* *Frige* or *Frea* amongst the Germanic peoples. Hence the confusion with *Frigg*. The Germanic and Scandinavian version become two deities by the Viking period.

Eh/Ehwaz

OERP

(eh) byþ for eorlum æþelinga wyn,
hors hōfum wlanc,
ðær him hæleþas ymb, welege on wicgum,
wrixlaþ spræce; and biþ unstyllum æfre frōfur.

Steed is nobleman's joy before heroes
a hoof-proud horse
where about it warriors
rich in stallions
exchange words

and is always a comfort to the restless

Garmonis medallion

Ehwaz means horse, an important cult animal and a symbol of sovereignty and power. Horses were also believed to possess otherworldly functions. Here the physical and spiritual weave almost inseparably, for the horse is a beast that could transition between worlds. Slepnir, Odin's eight legged steed, is a well known example. The importance of the horse to tribal society is reinforced in the presence of two runes that reflect the horse. Raido/rad is ride, inferring a journey and the horse is the physical, or metaphorical representation of the vehicle. Ehwaz offsets this individual interdependence with an emphasis on the communal value of horses.

In Celtic coins from across Gaul and Britain, and Germanic bracteate, horse motifs are often surrounded by celestial symbols. In Viking era mythology, two horses (*Skinfaxi* and *Hrimfaxi*) are said to pull the sun through the sky. This tradition is ancient, and echoed in Bronze age rock carvings and by the Trundholm horse, a cult image that portrays a horse pulling the sun.

This rune is absent from the later Younger Futhark inspired Viking poems. The idea that the horse is a comfort to the restless suggests the impetuousness of youthful warriors, the urge to gather a posse and head out. The OERP gives the impression here of a mounted war band. No doubt runic origins lay in warrior culture. Therefore the reference here recognises the social aspect of equestrianism, inferring a community, rather than *Raido's* solo endeavour. There is much less that is internal or introspective here. *Ehwaz* is external then, indicating the benefits of friendship and social gatherings.

References:

The Old English Rune Poem - Maureen Halsall

Runic Amulets & Magic Objects - Mindy Macleod and Bernard Mees

An Archaeology of Images - Miranda Alehouse Green

The Other Europe In The Middles Ages -Avars, Bulgar, Khazars & Cumans - Florin Curta & Roman Kovalev

Teutonic Mythology Vol III - Viktor Rydberg

A Reader In Comparative Indo-European Religion - Ranko Matasović

Runic & Hero Poems Of The Old Teutonic Peoples - Edited by Bruce Dickins

Mannaz/Mathr

OERP

*(man) byþ on myrgþe
his māgan lēof; sceal þēah ānra gehwylc
ōðrum swīcan, for ðām dryhten wyle
dōme sīne þæt earme flæsc eorþan betæcan.*

Man is clear to his kinsmen in mirth
yet each one must fail the others
since by his judgement the lord wishes
to commit the poor flesh to earth

OIRP

M er manns gaman ok moldar auki

Ok skipa skreytir

Man is man's pleasure
and mould's increase
and a ship's embellisher

ONRP

Maðr er moldar auki;
Mikil er græip á hauki

Man is mould's increase;
great is the grip of the hawk

Tacitus tells us in his book, Germania, how the ancient Germanic tribes believed their origins lay with a primeval earth god, known as Tuisto. He had a son called Mannus (man). This is paralleled in Vedic myth with the figure of Yama, a deified mortal, slain by his brother, Manu, the originator of mankind. The story of Kronos, and his disfigurement by his son, Zeus, follows the same pattern. All these archetypal rivalries point to a deep psychological phenomena, that of the son usurping the father.

The OERP flourishes this verse with overtly Christian sympathies. Christianity, in many ways, is a religion of death, and its worship. The suggestion is that we are a small part in a larger cosmological endeavour. What might at first appear a bleak prognosis in the rune poems reminds us of our mortality. Our existence must yield so that other forces can come into being. The OIRP's final line draws on ancient beliefs of ships as vessels that afforded passage to the otherworld. This poignant metaphor affirms the idea that though the physical state passes, and will break down into other states of physical existence, there is something else, whether we call it spirit, soul or energy, that moves on, into the beyond.

As in *Wyn*, knowing sorrow allows us to know true joy. The ultimate recognition of our mortality should allow us to cherish and celebrate life.

References:

The Old English Rune Poem - Maureen Halsall

A Reader In Comparative Indo - European Religion - Ranko Matasović

Tac., Germ. 10 - Winterbottom & Ogilvie 1975: 42; translation Mattingly 1970: 109

The Icelandic Rune Poem - R.I. Page

The Norwegian Rune Poem In Context: Style, Structure & Imagery - Veronka Szöke

Runic & Hero Poems of the Old Teutonic Peoples - Edited By Bruce Dickins

Laguz/Logr

OERP

*(lagu) byþ lēodum langsum geþūht,
gif hī sculun nēþun on nacan tealtum,
and hī sǣyþa swyþe brēgaþ,
and se brimhengest brīdles ne gymeð.*

Water is seemingly endless to men
if they must fare on a tilting ship
and sea-waves frighten them mightily
and the sea-steed does not heed the bridle

OIRP

L er vellandi vimur ok viðr ketill ok glommunga grund.

Sea is a welling water
a wide kettle
and a fish's field

ONRP

Logr er, fællr ór fjalle foss; en gull ero nosser.

A waterfall is a River falling out of a mountainside;
and costly ornaments are of gold.

Each poem treats this rune slightly differently. In the OERP the reference is to the ocean in turmoil, the ship is on a stormy sea and the voyagers are scared. They are in the hands of fate, specks on the broiling ocean. The ONRP possibly hints at the Volsung saga. The falls, where Loki deceives the dwarf, Andvari, and steals his gold, implies caution. The OIRP is stranger, and here hints at primal waters, specifically the bubbling waters of the mythical river Vimur. This is the river that Thor crossed on his way to see the giant, Geirröd. As Thor waded across the river, Gjálp, the giant's daughter, caused the river to surge. Standing on the banks, she unleashed a torrent of piss or menstrual fluid. However, Thor hurled a rock at her and thus blocked the swelling waters with her unconscious body. This hints at the latent enmity between this ancient sky-god and earthy giantesses.

*Njord**, the father god of the *Vanir,* and god of the ocean, is also suggested by this rune. He is an ancient deity, and is likely paired with *Nerthus*

(Njard). The masculine element is associated here with the ocean.

Here too I would place the runic stanza from *Sigrdrífumál*:

Wave-runes learn, if well thou wouldst shelter
The sail-steeds out on the sea;
On the stem shalt thou write, and the steering blade,
And burn them into the oars;
Though high be the breakers, and black the waves,
Thou shalt safe the harbour seek.

The OERP references the ocean as a force outwith human control, whilst the OIRP points out the importance of the sea as a resource. Just as agriculture provided much from the land (meat and crops) so too the ocean provided many resources (fish, walrus ivory, seal skins etc). In drawing this rune, the powerful elemental force of water and the value therein is invoked. In looking for metaphorical meaning, this could represent what is hidden beneath the surface that is of sufficient value to the seeker to brave being lost in the power of this element.

References:

Runic Amulets and Magic Objects - Mindy Macleod and Bernard Mees

Scandinavian Mythology - H.R Ellis

The Icelandic Rune Poem - R.I. Page

The Norwegian Rune Poem in Context: Style, Structure and Imagery - Veronka Szöke

The Old English Rune Poem - Maureen Halsall

Gods of the Ancient Northmen - Georges Dumezil

TheRoad to Hel - Hilda Roderick Ellis

A Reader In Comparative Indo-European Religion - Ranko Matasović

arild-hauge.com

Runic & Hero Poems of the Old Teutonic Peoples - edited by Bruce Dickins

* *Njordr* is derived from the PIE **ner-to-*, which means under/deep. By the Viking era the name of *Nerthus* was forgotten and thus myth told of how

Njord was married to a giantess, *Skadi*, who preferred the mountains, while he, after trying to live inland, moved back to *Nóatún*, his legendary abode. *Njord* is also a god of ships and place names attest to his worship down the Norwegian coast. Perhaps it is his giant form that grips a ship in his hands, holding it to the heavens, in rock art from the bronze-age. *Nóatún* literally means, enclosure of ships. *Njord* was probably linked to otherworld symbology, by this association. Ships were often vehicles for the dead to reach the afterlife. This train of thought is particularly ancient and many bronze age depictions of solar boats, and ritual vessels include giant figures, suggesting ancient gods such as *Njord/Nerthus*. Even in fairly recent times folklore recalls fishermen off the coast of Norway calling upon *'Njor'* to aid them with a hearty catch.

Ingwaz

OERP

(Ing) wæs ærest mid Ēast-Denum gesewen secgun,
oþ hē siððan ēst ofer wæg gewāt;
wæn æfter ran; ðus heardingas
ðone hæle nemdun.

Ing was first among the East Danes
seen by men until he later eastwards
went across the waves
the waggon sped behind them
thus the hard men named the hero.

The reference here is to Ing, the ancestor of the Danes, who went East across the Baltic. We only have the OERP to go by for this symbol. The reference to wagon may well refer to the type of ceremonial cart that was used by the Germanic peoples to transport effigies of their deities during festivals. Tacitus tells us of a tribe named the Ingavones, and the Danes were also sometimes referred to as the friends of Ing. Yngvi-Freyr, Snorri Sturlusson tells us, is another of Freyr's names. The eponymous tribe of the Ynglingar saga were his people.

Many tribes traced their lineage to divine ancestors. For example, the Lombards traced their lineage back to *Odin*. Adam of Bremen offers us a glimpse of the Norse city of Uppsala. Here, in a temple made of gold, three gods were worshipped, *Thor*, *Odin* and *Freyr*. Adam called *Freyr* by the appellation of *Fricco* and tells us that he dispenses wealth, peace and pleasure to mortals. *Freyr's* statue was also replete with a huge phallus, reinforcing his status as a god of virility. Every nine years, a festival was held to honour him at this temple. The aim of the festival was to unite the people and strengthen communal bonds.

Freyr means Lord, and his sister, *Freyja*, Lady. They are of the *Vanir*. These are the gentler family of deities who warred against the *Aesir*, and finally made peace with them. The pair appear as masculine and feminine aspects of harvests and fertility. While *Freyja's* realm is also the realm of love and passion, *Freyr* peacefully governed mortals and oversaw weddings. He is intrinsically bound to the farmstead community, and he was associated with the harvest as another of his names suggests, *inn fróði* (the prolific one).

Like all Norse deities, *Freyr* had magical tools. *Skinbladner* was his ship, forged by dwarves at *Loki's* instigation. This fabulous ship could hold all the warriors of *Asgard*, and yet *Freyr* could fold it and place it in his pocket. He also owned a golden boar, *Gullinborsti:* it is likely that this motif appears on shields and helmets to bring protection and luck in warfare.

Ing then functions as the seed, or progenitor of the people. Seed in an agricultural sense reminds us of *Freyr's* functions as a the god of harvest. This rune refers us to beginnings, followed by *Othalo*, which calls us back to honour our ancestry. In some versions of the pictogram for this rune, it resembles a seed, in the form of a diamond.

References:

The Old English Rune Poem - Maureen Halsall

European Paganism - Ken Dowden

Scandinavian Mythology - H.R Ellis

DAVE MIGMAN

Teutonic Mythology Vol I - Viktor Rydberg

Runic & Hero Poems of the Old Teutonic Peoples - Edited by Bruce Dickins

Othala

OERP

(ēþel) byþ oferlēof æghwylcum men,
gif he mōt ðær rihtes and gerysena
on brūcan on bolde blēadum oftast.

Homeland is very dear to every man
if there rightfully and with propriety
he may enjoy wealth in his dwelling generally.

This rune is sometimes written second from last, with Dagaz as the final. It appears this way in the OERP, and is followed by later runic symbols, added due to phonetic changes in OE. The OERP conjures a blissful scene of family and clan. What began with Feoh and the establishing of community ties has come full cycle to the return to the homeland, our roots and ancestry. It could conjure up images of those who have been separated through distance coming together again, returning with the spoils of conquest, or of daughters and sons returning to their ancestral homes having forged a new life elsewhere, bringing their knowledge and skills to show off to their elders. Positions of responsibility and power were often passed down through families, and strengthened through marital bonds.The concept of homecoming feels like the conclusion to a quest and metaphorically, this could represent the assimilation of the new into the established. It is a moving forward whilst being respectful of all that came before, the foundations on which a new way is built. Pictorially it echoes Ing as a seed, portraying the roots essential for growth. This works as a metaphor for family and ancestry.

Reference:

Runic & Hero Poems of The Old Teutonic Peoples - Edited by Bruce Dickins

Dagaz/Dæg

OERP

(dæg) byþ Drihtnes sond,
dēore mannum, mǣre Metodes lēoht,
myrgþ and tōhiht ēadgum and earmum,
eallum brīce.

Day is sent by the Lord,
   beloved by mankind, the glorious light of the Creator,
   a source of joy and hope to the haves and have-nots,
   of benefit to everyone.

In the OERP Dagaz appears after Othalo, completing the round with the breaking day. Here the reference exhibits overtly Christian imagery; harmony for all, and that the light's luminance is a relief from the dark of night. Thus the light of God confers a boon upon all. In this sense all are equal under the dome of the sky, for in the Christian sense, God loves all, those in the street and those in the castle.

This is another rune missing from the Younger Futhark. As regards the ancient, pre-christian world, in which the runic origins lay, a sun deity was different from one of the morning and evening light. Day as opposed to sun; the new day and the light that it brings. A solar symbol, but with reference to the cult of divine twins, known as the *Alcis*. These were personified as the morning and evening stars, demarcating the day. This pair find parallels in other Indo-European myths. In Vedic myth, the *Aśvinā* are the divine twins that are archetypes of the Greek *Dioskoúroi*, *Castor* and *Polydeukes* (*Castor & Pollux* of Roman myth). They are horsemen of salvation, who ride through the land, benign and helpful. They are renowned healers and physicians to the gods themselves. Tacitus describes the worship of the divine twins in a sacred grove, amongst a Germanic tribe known as the *Nahanarvali*. The ceremonies, on their behalf, were carried out by a transvestite priest. *Gemini* is the zodiacal recollection of such a widespread myth*.

Dagaz placed at the end of the set echoes the upbeat conclusion to each *ætt*. This reinforces the cyclical nature of the story of the runes - a new day comes and the cycle begins again.

It does work equally well outwith this sequence as a demarkation of a new beginning, following recognition of the ancestral beginnings in *Ing*. If the runes do indeed tell a linear story then the place of the new day is to suggest continuity and moving forward, beginning again and allowing the past to fall behind.

Reference:

Runelore - Edred Thorsson

The Old English Rune Poem - Maureen Halsall

European Paganism - Ken Dowden

Runic & Hero Poems of the Old Teutonic Peoples - Edited by Bruce Dickins

Gods and Myths of Northern Europe - H.R. Ellis-Davidson

The Meaning Of The Dokana - Margaret C. Waites

* Interestingly a sign associated with the *Dioskoúroi*, the '*Dokana*' appears to be an ancestor of the modern astrological symbol for this star sign. The *dokana* not only signifies the twins but also their place guarding the doorway between this world and the other. In this respect they retain their benevolent qualities as protectors. This symbol and the twins have been recognised on archaeological finds across Europe. In comparative myths the twins are usually sons of the thunder/sky god. This would bind them to *Thunor*, the ancient Germanic deity later known as Thor. The twins were depicted as young men. They are sometimes depicted as sun and moon, night and day, morning and evening and symbolised in many cultures by a double disc or pair of wheels.

STONE MAD RUNES

Urnes in Norway

Bibliography

Gods Of The Ancient Northmen - Geoges Dumèzil

Runelore - Edred Thorsson

The Rune Primer - Sweyn Plowright

Rudiments of Rune Lore - Stephen Pollington

Runes - Martin Findell

Runic Amulets & Magic Objects - Mindy Macleod and Bernard Mees

The Etymology of *Rune* - Bernard Mees (Royal Melbourne Institute of Technology)

Runes In The 1st Century - Bernard Mees

Language Isolates - Edited by Lyle Campbell

The Rune Primer - Sweyn Plowright

Rudiments of Runelore - Stephen Pollington

Names Of The u-Rune - Futhark Runic Studies vol 1 (2010) - Inmaculada Senra Silva

The Icelandic Rune Poem - R.I. Page

The Norwegian Rune Poem In Context: Style, Structure and Imagery - Veronka Szöke

The Old English Rune Poem - A Critical Edition - Maureen Halsall

Othin in England - J.S Ryan

Scandinavian Mythology - H.R Ellis

Contexts Of The Oldest Runic Inscriptions - Tineke Looijenga

The n-Rune & Nordic Charm Magic - Stephen A. Mitchell

The Road To Hel - Hilda Roderick Ellis

Corpus Poeticum Boreale Vol 1 & 2 - Gudbrand Vigfusson & F. York Powell

The Viking Way - Neil S. Price

Ancient Egyptian Literature; An Anthology - John L. Foster

Gods of Ancient Europe - Barbara Watterson

Celts & The Classical World - David Rankin

Encyclopaedia of Celtic mythology & Folklore - Patricia Monaghan

The Pagan Religions Of The Ancient British Isles - Ronald Hutton

The Celts, History, Life & Culture Vol 1 - Edited by, John T. Koch & Antone Minard

Celtic Culture; An historical Encyclopaedia - John T. Koch

Myths & Symbols In Pagan Europe - H.R Ellis Davidson

Tac., *Germ.* 10 = Winterbottom & Ogilvie 1975: 42; translation Mattingly 1970: 109

Ullr; A God On The Edge Of Memory - John Julian Molin

The Ancient Yew; A History of Taxus Baccata - Robert Beven Jones

Myth, Materiality & Lived Religion - (Edited) K.Wikstöm, P. Rova, A Nordberg, O. Sundquist, T. Zachrisson

Patterns in Comparative Religion - Mircea Eliade

Rites and Symbols of Initiation - Mircea Eliade

Slavic Myth - Mike Dixon Kennedy

An Encyclopaedia of the Barbarian world Vol 1 (8000B.C - 1000 A.D) - Peter Bogucki & Pam J. Crabtree (Editors)

An Archaeology of Images - Miranda Alehouse Green

The other Europe in the middles ages -Avars, bulgar, Khazars & Cumans - Florin Curta & Roman

Kovalev

Teutonic mythology Vol III - Viktor Rydberg

A reader In Comparative Indo-European Religion - Ranko Matasović

European Paganism - Ken Dowden

Teutonic mythology Vol I - Viktor Rydberg

Teutonic mythology Vol II - Viktor Rydberg

Runic & Hero Poems of the Old Teutonic Peoples - Edited by Bruce Dickins

Traces of Germanic Mythology from the 6-7th Century Carpathian Basin Based on Archaelogical Finds - Csaba Bálint

Old Norse Myth & Literature - Simonetta Battista

Norse Mythology - Mortensen and Crowell

Norse mythology; A Guide to the Gods, Heroes, Rituals & Beliefs - John Lindow

Eddic, Skaldic and Beyond: Poetic Variety in Medieval Iceland and Norway - Edited by Martin Chase

The Poetic Edda - Henry Adams Bellows

The Elder Eddas of Snorre Sturlusson - Edited by I.A Blackwell

The Folklore of Plants - T.F. Thiselton-Dyer

Irish Trees; Myths, Legends & Folklore - Niall Mac Coitir

Gods & Myths of Northern Europe - H.R. Ellis-Davidson

Gods of the Ancient Northmen - Georges Dumezil

The Origins of Runic Writing - Edited by Robert Mailhammer Theo Vennemann gen. Nierfeld and Birgit Anette Olsen

Heroic Identity In The World of Beowulf - Scott Gwara

Encyclopaedia of Norse & Germanic Folklore, Mythology & Magic - Claude Lecouteux

The Meaning Of The Dokana - Margaret C. Waites

Myths, Legends & Heroes - Edited - Daniel Anlezark

Celtic Cosmology & the Otherworld: Mythic Origins, Sovereignty & Liminality - Sharon Paice MacLeod

Inherited Bovine Aspects In Greek Reflexes Of The Indo-European Serpent-Slaying Myth - John Andrew McDonald

The Cult of Odin - Nora M. Chadwick

ABOUT THE AUTHOR

Dave Migman

Dave Migman was born in the wrong time. Despite this he continues to carve images into stone regardless of the invention of gentler artistic pursuits, such as origami. It is fueled by his passion for mythology and history and has enabled his wanderings across Europe. If you have ever happened upon Dave at his stall, you will know that he can talk for hours about the symbolism and significance of ancient times. His writing, both fiction and non fiction, reflects the dearth of research he has done - not unlike the carvings he creates, he goes beneath the surface to uncover the truth that lies within. He is also a thoroughly good bloke but please don't feed him after midnight.

Please check out his blog and also subscribe to receive more information about Dave's subsequent writing.

Made in the USA
Las Vegas, NV
18 January 2021